GRESLEY'S
D49s

PETER TUFFREY

GREAT NORTHERN

ACKNOWLEDGEMENTS

I would like to thank the following people for their help: Roger Arnold, David Burrill, John Chalcraft, Paul Chancellor, Peter Crangle, D.J. Dippie, John Law, Hugh Parkin, Rail Online, Bill Reed, G.T. Robinson, Andrew, Rachel and Sue Warnes, David P. Williams.

Gratitude should also be expressed to my son Tristram Tuffrey for his help throughout the project.

Unless otherwise stated all photographs from the author's collection.

Great Northern Books Limited
PO Box 1380, Bradford, BD5 5FB
www.greatnorthernbooks.co.uk

ISBN: 978-1-914227-25-7

Design and layout: David Burrill

CIP Data
A catalogue for this book is available from the British Library

INTRODUCTION

Entering traffic during the glorious years of the London & North Eastern Railway, Sir Nigel Gresley's D49 Class 4-4-0 is arguably a forgotten part of both the designer's and company's history. The locomotives served a dual purpose of taking over from older pre-Grouping designs, which were outdated and uneconomical, whilst providing large-scale comparative data between piston and poppet valves. At the time, the latter valves and operating gear had seen limited use by the company.

Throughout his career, Gresley hoped to improve the efficiency of the steam locomotive and the poppet valve offered this over the other type. Yet, a successful application to the railways was elusive and, despite several other gambles by Gresley, the D49s so-fitted remained the only LNER poppet valve engines for their lifetime. The class was left to work on in the North East and Scotland until the late 1950s when withdrawals commenced. One was subsequently preserved and serves as a lone representative of a bold attempt to move the steam locomotive forward as well as a relic from a lost era of transport in Britain.

The journey to the birth of the D49 Class began in the early 20th century as the practice of superheating steam began to receive attention and popularity. This was a process where saturated steam was fed back into the boiler through superheater elements thereby increasing the temperature and reducing the amount of water vapour. With steam at a higher temperature, more work was done from smaller amounts due to volume increases and the heat present in the boiler was employed more efficiently. Yet, a problem arose with the addition of a superheater to existing locomotive designs that mainly used slide valves. The higher temperature caused issues with the lubricating oil used for the valves and increased wear, which was already an issue. As a result, many designers switched over to piston valves and these also had improved valve events to further increase efficiency, though a tendency to wear still existed.

Late in the 19th century, poppet valves were developed for use in stationary steam engines. Whereas slide and piston valves travel over inlet and exhaust ports, poppet valves lift off their seats – there are two connected – allowing steam in and out of the cylinder. The type offered the advantage of better port openings, improved steam flow and drastically reduced wear, whilst requiring little lubrication. Dr Hugo Lenz (a South-African-born Austrian engineer) worked on developing the poppet valve in power station steam engines before moving to the locomotive application. He first applied this to a small group of Grand Duchy of Oldenburg State Railway engines and was successful enough to find use on others used by the company.

Lenz (sometimes stylised as Lentz) entered into an agreement for his arrangement of poppet valves for locomotives to be marketed and distributed by the British company Davey, Paxman & Co. in the early 1920s. Though likely aware of poppet valve developments, Gresley was perhaps prompted by this event to experiment with the valves. Shortly after Grouping, Gresley made the first enquiries and by May 1925 the pioneer British locomotive with poppet valves was J20 Class 0-6-0 no. 8280. This belonged to an ex-Great Eastern Railway design of A.J.

Hill's, the D81 Class. Oscillating cam valve gear was used, being one of two options, with the other rotary cam valve gear. No. 8280 had the poppet valves housed in chests bolted to the top of the two inside cylinders and the existing Stephenson motion was adapted to move the oscillating cams. Following trials, no. 8280 was found to have an economy in coal consumption, whilst being in service for nearly 20,000 miles more between general repairs than the average for the J20 Class.

Buoyed by this initial experience, Gresley followed up by equipping a passenger locomotive with poppet valves. Another GER design was altered – S.D. Holden's B12 (GER S69) Class 4-6-0 – and no. 8516 entered service with the modification in December 1926. A slight difference from the initial experiment was no. 8516 which had valve chest and cylinders cast together. The results from this also showed a slight improvement on coal consumption, though the maintenance time was not as marked. Five more class members received poppet valves to the end of the decade, whilst ten new B12s erected had the equipment from new.

In the meantime, traffic requirements in the North East and Scotland called for a new secondary express passenger locomotive. Gresley delegated the task of detail work to Darlington drawing office, though the main stipulation was for the engine to use three cylinders in a 4-4-0 chassis, with the diagram 97 boiler, which at the time was being fitted to J39 Class 0-6-0s. The first order was placed at Darlington in April 1926 and consisted of twenty-eight D49s. Initially, twenty-six of these were to be fitted with piston valves and two were to be compounds, though few details of the latter exist. In mid-summer, Gresley changed the order to include six with oscillating cam poppet valves. Several months were taken to develop the application, allowing all twenty piston valve engines to be constructed at Darlington from October 1927 to May 1928. When ready, the valves were again bolted to the tops of the cylinders and numbered four with each of the three cylinders. The cam was oscillated from a short arm connected to the outside motion, whilst for the inside cylinder Gresley's '2 to 1' lever had to be moved from the front to rear and operated vertically rather than horizontally as standard. This provided a benefit of reducing the amount of dirt and ash from the smokebox contaminating the components which led to excessive wear in the joints.

At the end of August 1928 when twenty-six of the order had been built – the other two did not appear until the following year – the Scottish Area had been sent 15 locomotives and the North Eastern Area 11. All but one of the oscillating cam engines were sent to sheds in the latter region (Neville Hill and York), perhaps to keep them close for works attention, which was soon needed. A fault in the valve gear caused the failure of a component and resulted in the '2 to 1' lever being switched to the horizontal which improved matters. The Scottish engines fared better, but a minor alteration was necessary for the crews who disliked the North Eastern-type steam reverse gear and preferred the normal screw-type. Otherwise, the locomotives ably carried out their duties at Edinburgh Haymarket, Perth, Dundee and Edinburgh St Margaret's sheds. These mainly consisted of inter-city passenger trains, often double-heading, either with a classmate, an ex-North British Railway 4-4-0 or 'Atlantic'.

Whilst the oscillating cam engines were satisfactory, Gresley aimed for improvements by using a rotary cam valve gear. Even before the appearance of the six oscillating engines, he had requested a rotary cam design from the manufacturers and the work was approved in early 1927. No. 8280 was test-fitted with the equipment and ran nearly 5,000 miles without trouble allowing progress to be made on the D49 application. Work continued through 1928 and was finally completed in early 1929, with no. 352 *Leicestershire* in service from March and no. 336 *Buckinghamshire* completed during June. The rotary motion for the camshaft came from a return crank on the leading pair of coupled wheels connected to bevel gears and a driveshaft. The cams had profiles for five rates of cut-off in forward gear – 15, 25, 35, 50 and 75% – and two for reverse – 35 and 75%.

A further eight piston valve engines were ordered in 1928 and built during the following year. At the end of 1929, Gresley was evidently satisfied enough with the rotary cam design to perpetuate the application on the D49s by a further 15. Tests conducted around this time between all three variants showed the rotary cam valve gear to be more economical in the working of the engine, with the oscillating cam performance similar to a standard piston valve D49, but later trials saw the gap between rotary cam and piston valve engines reduced. Nevertheless, in late 1933 Gresley ordered the final 25 D49 Class locomotives with rotary cam gear, whilst also starting construction of P2 Class 2-8-2 no. 2001 *Cock o' the North*, which was his final 'fling' with the arrangement.

The D49 Class reached 76 members in February 1935 with all 28 piston valve locomotives in Scotland and the remainder in the North East, York, Hull and Leeds. The piston valve and oscillating cam engines all received names of counties – colloquially referred to as 'Shires' – and the rotary cam poppet valve engines took those of Hunt meetings, with the original pair renamed in 1932.

Despite the other LNER locomotives fitted with poppet valves having them removed by the late 1930s, the apparatus persisted throughout for the rotary cam engines, but the oscillating cam engines had them replaced when cylinder renewals were necessary in the late 1930s. Apart from detail changes, the main visible difference in D49 engines was the switch in tender types which began just before the war. The Group Standard 4,200-gallon tender was paired to all from new in two varieties: stepped-out top; straight-sided. As this type had a water scoop that the D49 did not necessarily need, old North Eastern Railway-type tenders with coal rails were switched with several class members and the Group Standard tenders went to new V2 Class 2-6-2s. During the early 1940s, a number of Great Central Railway tenders were displaced from 0-8-0s being converted into tank shunters and these found themselves connected to D49s. These had stepped side sheets, though two had coal rails.

Another visual change concerned the livery. The D49s started with LNER apple green passenger livery, then during the war plain black was used on all locomotives for economy. After the war, black livery remained and British Railways only added lining rather than restoring passenger green livery. The original numbers of the D49 Class also changed. At first provided using gaps in the North Eastern Area's stock list, Edward Thompson wanted order brought to the fleet and provided blocks, starting with express passenger and moving down to freight shunters. The number range taken by the D49s was 2700-2775. After Nationalisation, British Railways devised another renumbering system and decreed 60,000 be added to existing LNER numbers.

An even greater change could have occurred had Thompson's reconstruction plan come to fruition. No. 365 *The Morpeth* was rebuilt from rotary cam valve gear to piston valves with two inside cylinders during the early 1940s as a prototype for the project. Under tests, the engine proved inferior to the other D49s, as well as contemporary 4-4-0s and was cast into the wilderness, relatively speaking. The engine went on to be the victim of a 'rough shunt' in the early 1950s and scrapped as a result.

A useful change could have occurred under BR as experiments were conducted with the infinitely variable valve gear used with no. 361 *The Garth* (later no. 62764). The limitations of the five-step camshaft was apparent early on and tests with a seven-step arrangement did not progress, whilst mechanical problems were encountered with an infinitely variable camshaft leading to an early discontinuation. BR resurrected the latter and tested the locomotive at Rugby, though interest in the project was insufficient for real developments to take place. *The Garth* remained equipped with this until withdrawal and does not appear to have experienced any adverse effects.

The D49s worked relatively in the background throughout the BR period, though were sometimes at the head of important trains, such as the Liverpool-Newcastle intercity service when running through North and West Yorkshire, as well as the Hull portion of the 'Yorkshire Pullman' between there and Doncaster. Though at the main depots under the LNER, the introduction of new classes, such as Thompson B1s, led to displacements to other depots and local trains were more typical of their later history. Particularly towards the late 1950s, employment could be hard to find for the class and several were stored out of service for periods. This likely resulted in the decision to begin the withdrawal process relatively early and the first went in 1957. All had gone by 1961 and Darlington Works scrapyard disposed of a large number of D49s. With this quick demise, the D49s perhaps did not enjoy a surge of interest as many other classes did which survived longer to the last days of steam in 1967 and 1968. Thankfully, one enthusiast was devoted enough to pursue no. 246 *Morayshire* and the locomotive was initially presented to a museum. Subsequently, a return to steam was made, though in recent years much overhaul work has kept the engine on the sidelines. While this is the case, hopefully this collection of superb colour and black-and-white images serves to highlight the class and remind why a return to steam is important for the surviving engine to represent an interesting class for Gresley, the LNER and BR.

Peter Tuffrey
Doncaster, May 2022

LNER

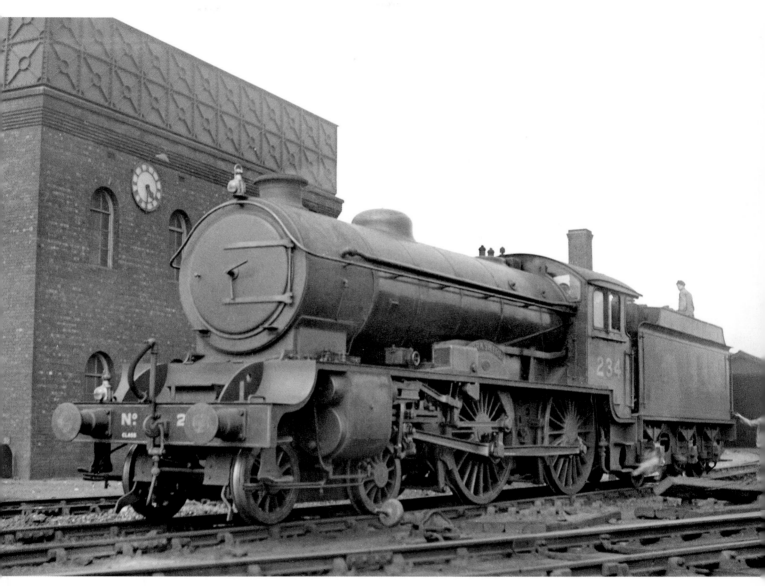

Above NO. 234 – LEEDS NEVILLE HILL SHED

The first Gresley D49 Class 4-4-0 was also the first LNER passenger locomotive to be designed from new specifically for the company. No. 234 *Yorkshire* was this engine and completed at Darlington Works in late October 1927. Initially, no. 234 was selected to work at York, yet the locomotive was on the ex-Great Central Railway main line from Gorton until the end of the year when transferred to Leeds Neville Hill shed. This is the location for this image taken in the yard during 1928. No. 234 remained employed there to just before World War Two when moved to Hull. Photograph courtesy Rail Photoprints.

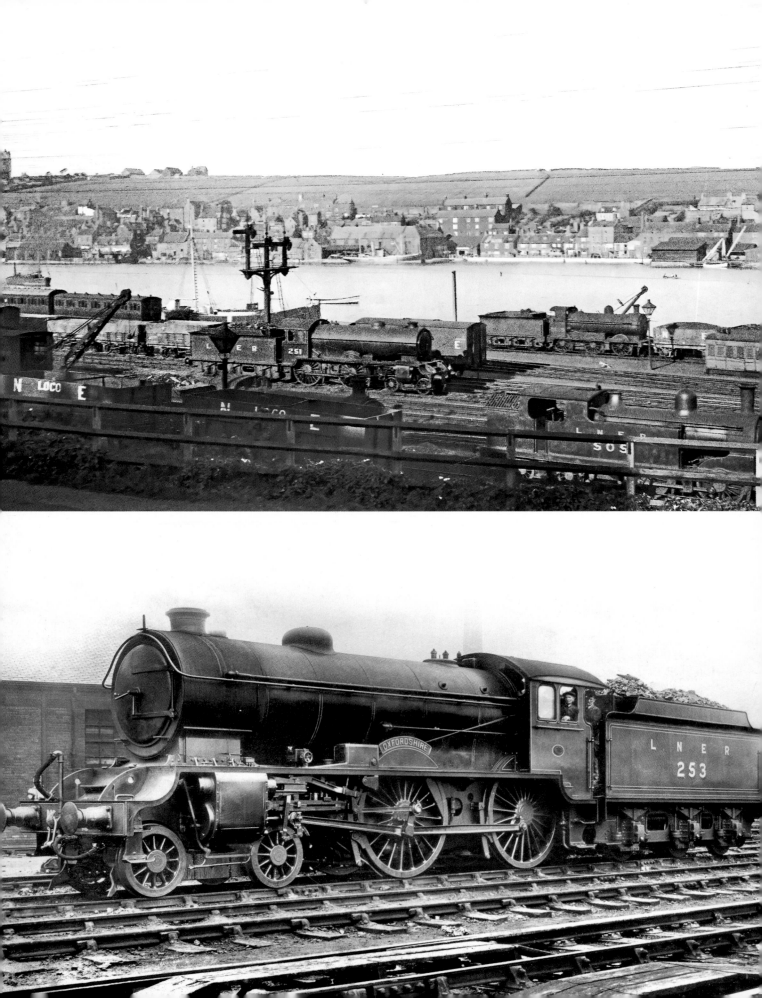

Above **NO. 256 – YORK STATION**

The fourth D49 to enter service was no. 256 *Hertfordshire* in early December 1927. At this time the engine's number would have been positioned on the tender (see below) but has subsequently moved to the cab side, which likely occurred at the first general repair at Darlington in late 1929/early 1930. No. 256 was noted later in the year returning for attention following a collision. The locomotive is at York station, probably during the early 1930s. An ex-Lancashire & Yorkshire Railway engine, George Hughes Class 8 4-6-0 no. 10421, is at the next platform. This engine was in service to November 1934. Photograph courtesy Rail-Online.

Opposite above **NO. 251 – WHITBY SHED**

Many railway companies paid little thought to implementing an orderly numbering scheme. When the D49s were introduced, the new locomotives were placed in gaps available, so after no. 234 *Yorkshire* followed no. 251 *Derbyshire*. The latter was in traffic almost a month after no. 234 and went to work at Leeds Neville Hill. Around 1938, no. 251 has travelled to Whitby and is in the shed yard for servicing. Worsdell G5 Class 0-4-4T no. 505 is also present. Photograph from the Chris Davies Collection courtesy Rail Photoprints.

Opposite below **NO. 253**

After the formation of the LNER, the company's initials were placed on the tender side above the locomotive's number. This continued for several years until the late 1920s when 'LNER' took the tender side and the engine number moved to the cab side. No. 253 *Oxfordshire* has the first arrangement at an unidentified location during the late 1920s. New to Neville Hill, by mid-1928 the locomotive was at York and this spell lasted four years. Also of note is the Darlington maker's plate positioned on the cab side and lining has been applied.

Above NO. 265 – GALASHIELS STATION

The Midland and North British Railway companies ran an Edinburgh to St Pancras train via Carlisle before Grouping and this continued under the LNER/LMSR. In the late 1920s, the principal train was christened the 'Thames-Forth Express' and the southbound train departed at 10.00 for arrival in London at 19.20. A St Pancras-bound train is at Galashiels station c. 1934 with no. 265 *Lanarkshire*. A Pullman carriage appears to be in the formation. Photograph courtesy Rail Photoprints.

Opposite above NO. 264 – COWLAIRS

The Edinburgh & Glasgow Railway was met with strong objections from canal interests when approaching Glasgow. A tunnel and incline were necessary to bypass this obstacle, though in reaching Queen Street station the company provided an equally daunting challenge. The incline was severely graded, up to 1 in 41 for over a mile, and required assistance from rope haulage from opening in the early 1840s up to the early 20th century. Even then, a locomotive was often employed to assist at the rear of trains ascending the bank and no. 264 *Stirlingshire* has one here in the late 1920s. New in mid-December 1927, the locomotive was sent to Edinburgh Haymarket shed and this express is likely bound for the city. The ascent of the incline was often a dramatic occurrence as depicted and a group appear to be watching the action from the bridge in the background. Photograph courtesy Rail Photoprints.

Opposite below NO. 266 – DUNDEE SHED

No. 266 *Forfarshire* stands outside Dundee shed in July 1932. The locomotive was nearly five years old at this point and was sent new from Darlington to the depot. A further five joined no. 266 and the contingent worked main line duties from Dundee. Early in the Second World War, *Forfarshire* transferred to Edinburgh Haymarket. As Gresley Pacifics did not work between Edinburgh and Aberdeen until the early 1930s, the D49s were often double-headed with North British Railway Reid Class H Atlantics or Robinson D11 Class 4-4-0 'Directors' on heavy trains.

Above NO. 246 – FORTH BRIDGE

A local train for Edinburgh crosses the Firth of Forth behind no. 246 *Morayshire* on 20th August 1937. The engine was dispatched from Darlington to Dundee in February 1928 and employed there for two years. A transfer to Perth occurred at this time and no. 246 did not move again until March 1944 when taken on at Haymarket. Note the reversed headboard for a named train carried below the smokebox.

Opposite above NO. 270 AND NO. 306 – COWLAIRS

Both no. 270 *Argyllshire* and no. 306 *Roxburghshire* were new to the Scottish Area at Edinburgh Haymarket and St Margaret's depot respectively. At this time – early 1928 – the D49s were provided with sanding when running forward only. By 1933, experience in service resulted in Scottish engines, i.e. those working out of Glasgow Queen Street station up Cowlairs incline, being equipped with sanding for rearward travel as well. No. 270 and no. 306 have a train on Cowlairs bank in 1928 – note both have entered traffic with LNER and their number on the tender. Photograph courtesy Rail Photoprints.

Opposite below NO. 236 – CROFT SPA

The LNER inherited a complicated arrangement of brake systems upon the formation of the company in 1923. Two of the constituent companies – the Great Central and Great Northern Railways – used vacuum and steam brakes for different applications, whilst the other four – Great Eastern, Great North of Scotland, North British and North Eastern Railways – favoured Westinghouse air brakes. Both systems had advantages and drawbacks to their use, though the LNER decided in the late 1920s to concentrate on vacuum and steam brakes. As the early D49s were built on the cusp of this decision and their sphere of operation was the North Eastern and North British Areas, the locomotives were new with Westinghouse brakes and vacuum ejectors. The equipment is present here on the running plate of no. 236 *Lancashire* which is with an express at Croft Spa in May 1932. The engine switched over to steam and vacuum at the end of the year.

Above NO. 310 – EDINBURGH HAYMARKET SHED

A feature of the early engines was the Wakefield 6-feed mechanical lubricator located on the running plate of the left-hand side of the locomotive. This fed just the piston valves as the axleboxes received oil from the cab. The feeds for the piston valves were later altered to include the two outside cylinders. Subsequent D49s received superior mechanical lubricators to remedy this defect. The outside cylinders of the early engines also had short drain pipes and this was again later modified to use longer pipes. No. 310 *Kinross-shire* is at Edinburgh Haymarket shed during 1929. Holmes J36 Class 0-6-0 no. 9775 is in the yard on the left, whilst behind stands a Gresley Pacific with corridor tender.

Opposite above NO. 250

From 1862, the premier train for the East Coast companies was the 'Flying Scotsman' express between King's Cross and Edinburgh Waverley. Whilst mainly known as running between those two places, portions of the train were destined for elsewhere. Under the LNER, carriages were present for Glasgow, Perth and Aberdeen, though latterly vehicles were largely for the 'Granite City'. Gresley's A1/A3 Pacifics were used on the East Coast Main Line, yet between Edinburgh and Aberdeen weight limits restricted their use to the mid-1930s. No. 250 *Perthshire* has the 'Flying Scotsman' headboard here in the early 1930s at an unidentified location (likely either Perth or Dundee), having worked one of the through portions. The locomotive was new to Perth shed in March 1928 and remained to 1951.

Opposite below NO. 307 – DUNDEE SHED

Seen at Dundee shed in July 1932, no. 307 *Kincardineshire* was fresh from a general repair at Darlington Works a month earlier. At this time, the engine is noted as having the cylinders replaced, which was a costly process as Darlington adopted Vincent Raven's practice of using a 'monobloc' casting comprising all three cylinders when producing the D49 Class. Adding to potential problems was the fact lubrication was not provided to the cylinders initially, but this was later rectified for the outside pair only. Features of note here are the livery and lining applied to the cylinder side, which was Darlington practice, the front footsteps – present starting from no. 307 when new but not preceding engines – and the box on top of the running plate. This latter had no function apart from being decorative in covering the expansion link of the valve gear. No. 307 was allocated to Dundee from new.

Above NO. 320

The oscillating cam valve gear was housed in boxes mounted above the three cylinders. Four valves were present for allowing steam to enter and exit the cylinder. These were controlled by a camshaft driven by a rocking arm taking energy from the outside valve gear. Whilst the piston valve locomotives had the Gresley '2 to 1' lever mounted horizontally behind the cylinders, the oscillating cam engines had this in the same position but vertically. No. 320 *Warwickshire* was the second engine with oscillating cam valve gear built at Darlington in late May 1928. The locomotive's first allocation was to York and this could be the location for the above image taken when fitted with the motion. Removal occurred in early 1938.

Opposite above NO. 318 – DARLINGTON

The first of the poppet valve D49s appeared several months after the first standard engine owing to the development necessary for the equipment. No. 318 *Cambridgeshire* was the pioneer when entering traffic from Darlington in May 1928 and was employed at Leeds Neville Hill shed. Soon after, imperfections in the valve gear were found to be causing stresses at the end of the valve connecting rod which resulted in the failure of the component. Within a year the decision was made to restore Gresley's '2 to 1' lever to the horizontal, making a clear difference to the incident rate and the six engines were soon changed. No. 318 was the second engine to be treated at the first general repair in February 1930. Here, the locomotive has an express at Darlington in May 1932.

Opposite below NO. 311

The final engine from the original order for twenty piston valve D49s was no. 311 *Peebles-shire*. When completed at Darlington in May 1928, the engine joined the stock at St Margaret's. According to RCTS *Locomotives of the LNER Part 4*, no. 311 was assigned to a specific crew and often on the 18.29 train from Edinburgh to Carlisle which was a difficult proposition owing to stops and the nature of the line. The D49s working from St Margaret's had a wide sphere of operation, including the Waverley route, to Newcastle, Dundee and Perth. No. 311 is at an unidentified location, likely during the 1930s.

Above NO. 327 – DONCASTER SHED

Standing in the yard at Doncaster shed on 14th April 1935 is no. 327 *Nottinghamshire*. The engine had undergone two changes to this point: '2 to 1' lever change in June 1930; and steam and vacuum brakes replaced Westinghouse in March 1932. Several further modifications took place subsequently. No. 327 had worked to Doncaster from Hull and appears to have been at the front of a special, with a number card attached to the centre lamp iron. Resting on the right is Gresley K3 Class 2-6-0 no. 1154. The locomotive was new in May 1931 and later under BR mainly worked on the GC Section. Photograph courtesy Rail Photoprints.

Opposite below NO. 327

An early view of no. 327 *Nottinghamshire*, likely taken at York in 1928/1929. Darlington produced the locomotive in July 1928 and a number of the as-built features are present: '2 to 1' lever cover; Westinghouse brake equipment; number and lettering placed on the tender side; short cylinder drain pipes. No. 327 was at York until 1932 when transferred to Hull Botanic Gardens and remained in the city until condemned in January 1961.

Above **NO. 335**

In late August 1928 Darlington delivered no. 335 *Bedfordshire* for service to York shed and this could be the location for this image from the 1930s. The date is post-May 1930 when the '2 to 1' lever was returned to the horizontal as a small box cover in front of the mechanical lubricator (above the trailing bogie wheel) has been removed. This covered the lever in a similar manner to a larger one over the expansion link. No. 335 moved on to Hull Botanic Gardens in 1932 and was at Bridlington from 1935 until just before the Second World War when returning to Hull.

Above **NO. 336 – YORK SHED**

The installation of the 500-ton mechanical coaler was still a year away when no. 336 *Buckinghamshire* was pictured at York shed's coal stage in 1931. No. 336 was the second of the rotary cam-equipped D49s and was in service three months after no. 352 at the start of June 1929. Stabled at York initially, no. 336 deputised for no. 329 *Inverness-shire* at Perth shed when problems were experienced with that engine. Returning to England in early 1931, the locomotive was at York from then until 1938. During this period, no. 336 was renamed *The Quorn* in May 1932.

Opposite above **NO. 329 – GLASGOW EASTFIELD SHED**

No. 329 *Inverness-shire* is in as-new condition during 1928 whilst at Glasgow Eastfield shed – a Reid J35 Class 0-6-0, no. 973X, is also in the yard. The D49 Class locomotive has the vertical '2 to 1' lever, Westinghouse brakes and number on the tender. First allocated to Perth, no. 329 had been employed there for several weeks when the problem with the centre cylinder was noticed and the engine returned south for observation which led to the change in position of Gresley's lever. Back in Scotland at Perth during late summer 1929, *Inverness-shire*'s centre cylinder failed again, resulting in further tests. From York, where the locomotive was based during both spells, the engineers decided the cut-off had to be restricted to 62% from 65% and a tight control of the loads handled was necessary. Glasgow Eastfield became no. 329's home when given the all-clear to be used in revenue-earning service in early 1931. Photograph from the David P. Williams Colour Archive.

Opposite below **NO. 352 – YORK SHED**

Apparently receiving attention (note the components on the buffer beam) inside York shed during the mid-1930s is no. 352 *The Meynell*. The engine was the first of the initial order for two D49s fitted with rotary cam operated valve gear when built in March 1929. At this time, no. 352 was named *Leicestershire* following the original naming scheme. In the early 1930s, the policy changed to established fox hunting groups and no. 352 was altered to conform. From June 1932, it became *The Meynell* after the hunt in Leicestershire. The engine was York-allocated for a number of years.

Above NO. 2756 – COWLAIRS

As mentioned, the LNER's numbering for new locomotives filled in gaps left in the stock list. Following the construction of Gresley's new A3 Class Pacifics in 1929, taking nos 2743 to 2752, the second order for eight piston valve D49s was allocated nos 2753 to 2760. No. 2756 *Selkirkshire* has ascended Cowlairs incline in 1930, with a particularly long train following behind. The local shed at Eastfield (just to the north of the engine here behind the camera) took no. 2756 onto the roster from new in March 1929 to March 1937. Photograph courtesy Rail Photoprints.

Opposite above NO. 2753 – GLASGOW EASTFIELD JUNCTION

No. 2753 *Cheshire* passes a track gang at work near Glasgow Eastfield shed, close to Cowlairs Works, with an express in 1929. The engine was new in traffic from February of this year and initially allocated to Eastfield depot. This was only briefly, as a transfer to Perth occurred at the end of March. No. 2753 returned to Glasgow in July, being employed at the shed for the next fourteen years. Photograph courtesy Rail Photoprints.

Opposite below NO. 2755 – GLASGOW EASTFIELD SHED

The area of Springburn, north of Glasgow centre, was particularly heavily industrialised. The main workshops were railway-related, with the North British and Caledonian Railways establishing Cowlairs and St Rollox Works respectively, whilst the North British Locomotive Company's two shops were sited in between. The NBR and CR also built locomotive depots, with the aforementioned founding Eastfield shed north of Cowlairs in 1904. This was a large through-road building with 14 lines, a coal stage and two turntables, one in the north-east corner and another on the southern edge. No. 2755 *Berkshire* is on the last mentioned in September 1929. The engine was six months old at this point and the first employment was at Eastfield. A move to Carlisle occurred in 1936. Photograph courtesy Rail Photoprints.

NO. 2759 – COWLAIRS
An express, with leading clerestory-roof vehicles, has just tackled Cowlairs bank with no. 2759 *Cumberland* in 1935. Photograph courtesy Rail Photoprints.

Above NO. 2757 – GLASGOW EASTFIELD SHED

Resting in the yard at Glasgow Eastfield shed during August 1932 is no. 2795 *Dumfries-shire*. Note the locomotive has the long cylinder drain pipes and the painted and lined cylinder block is still distinct.

Below NO. 2759 – EDINBURGH HAYMARKET SHED

In the company of a Gresley A1 Pacific at Edinburgh Haymarket on 1st August 1937 is no. 2759 *Cumberland*. Photograph by Les Hanson from the David Hanson Archive courtesy Rail-Online.

Above NO. 201 – LEEDS

With no. 336 and no. 352, which had the rotary motion, deemed a success in comparison to the oscillating cam engines, an order of 15 new D49s with rotary cam valve gear was placed in December 1929 for construction at Darlington. Owing to the severe trade depression, this did not begin until early 1932 and no. 201 *The Bramham Moor* was the first in traffic during mid-April. Pictured in Leeds at this time (almost certainly at Neville Hill shed) the new engine is admired by Supervisory Foreman A. Cartwright, Shed Foreman H. Broscombe, Cleaner D. Metcalfe, Shed Labourer J. Stanhope and Fireman A. Benson. The *LNER Magazine* for May 1932 carried the information that the new locomotives: '…will be named after famous hunts in the territory served by the L.N.E.R. [and] are to be provided with a new design of name-plate, surmounted by a fox…The new locomotives will be noteworthy as the first of any railway to bear the names of famous hunts. The choice is as appropriate as the naming of the famous "Flying Scotsman" Pacifics after racehorses. A locomotive that carries a name as well as a number is more distinctive and possesses a greater publicity value than the engine that is distinguished by an unromantic set of numerals. But the name should be appropriate and this is so in the case of names of racehorses and hunts, for speed is the implication and speed after all is to the public the leading feature of an express passenger locomotive. The introduction of a fox on the nameplate is a happy and original idea and furthers the implication of speed.'

Opposite above NO. 211 – YORK STATION

Water is about to be taken from a platform column at York station. No. 211 *The York and Ainsty* is the engine at the head of the express.

Opposite below NO. 235 – YORK SHED

An engineman is in the pit underneath no. 235 *The Bedale* in June 1934 as part of preparations to allow the locomotive to work the next train from York station.

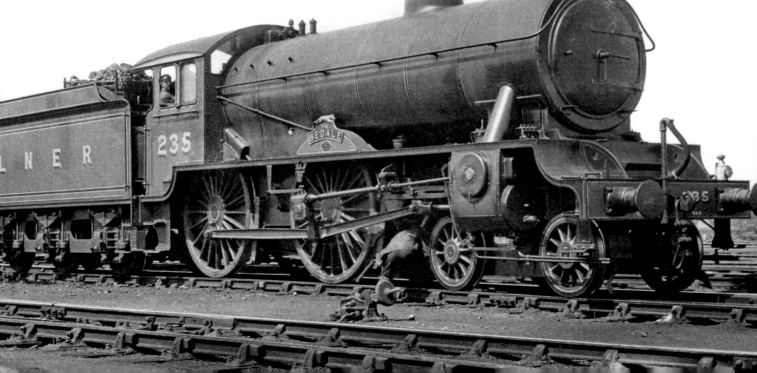

Above NO. 247 – DARLINGTON

No. 247 *The Blankney* is under the final preparations for a return to traffic following a general repair at Darlington in October 1937. Only the final few D49s were provided with steam heating when new and the other class members were fitted retrospectively. This began in the mid-1930s and was completed before the start of the Second World War. No. 247 had the connection installed at the front end during this visit to the works. From new in July 1932 until 1940 no. 247 was allocated to York shed.

Opposite above NO. 235 – YORK SHED

When new, the D49s had the LNER's apple green livery, which was standard for express passenger locomotives, and this was lined with black and white. The number on the cab side and the company's initials on the tender were applied in 12-in.-high transfers in gold with black and red shading. The number was present on the buffer beam in a smaller, yet similar style, whilst the engine's classification was also displayed. During the war, as a cost- and labour-saving measure, all locomotives were painted black. Following the conflict, LNER green returned for some passenger engines, though the D49s missed out and were later allocated mixed traffic black livery, with cream, grey and red lining under British Railways. A number plate was also fixed to the smoke box door. No. 235 *The Bedale* gleams at York shed in 1938. Towards the end of the year, the locomotive underwent a general repair at Darlington and at this time a steam heating capability for carriages was provided. Photograph H.M. Lane courtesy Colour-Rail.

Opposite below NO. 269 – KIRBY MOORSIDE

The Gilling & Pickering Railway was promoted in the mid-1860s to reach the area to the north of the Thirsk & Malton Railway line which had been bypassed. Construction started in the early 1870s and was ready in stages to the full opening in 1875. Kirby Moorside station (the town is spelled Kirkbymoorside) accepted the first train on 1st January 1874 and was one of two passing points on the single-track line. Token working was enforced along the length of the route, which left the T&MR at Gilling, and the signalling had been recently upgraded when no. 269 *The Cleveland* was caught about to exchange the token at Kirby Moorside in August 1937. Renamed Kirbymoorside after Nationalisation, passenger services survived at the station until 1953 and the line finally closed in 1964. The station house survived until recently when demolished. Photograph courtesy Colour-Rail.

NO. 288 – YORK STATION
With 'Scarborough Flier' headboard, no. 288 *The Percy* is at York station in the 1930s.

Above **NO. 282 – DONCASTER STATION**
A southbound freight train is at Doncaster station behind no. 282 *The Hurworth*.

Below **NO. 283 – DONCASTER STATION**
Another D49 is seen at Doncaster station. In this instance, no. 283 *The Middleton* stands at the platform with a passenger train, with leading clerestory coach, during the 1930s. New to York, the engine was also at Heaton, Hull, and Leeds Neville Hill during the decade.

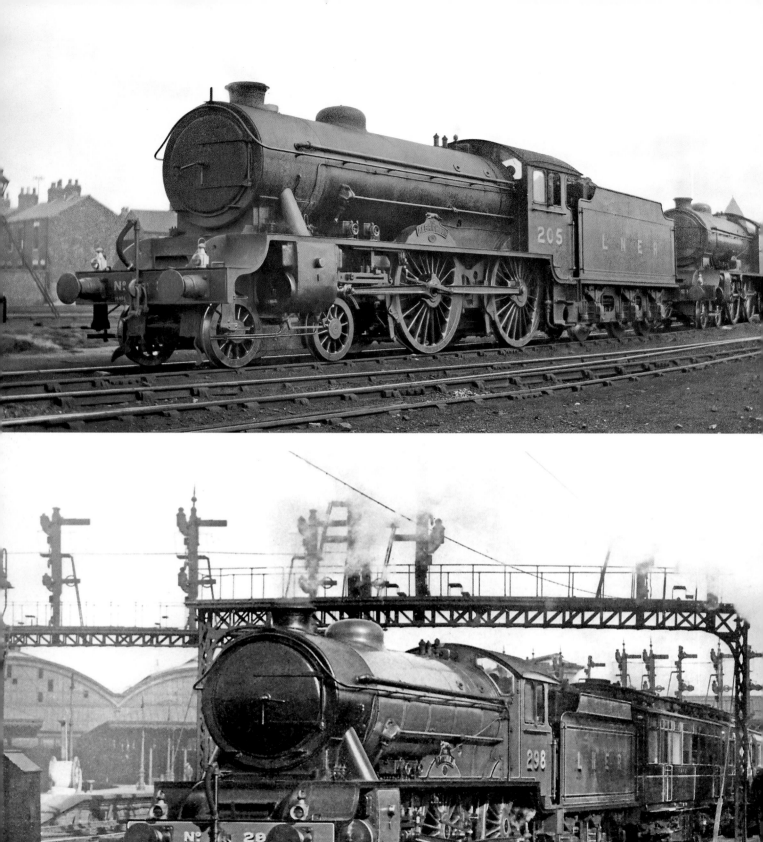

Above NO. 297 – MICKLEFIELD

East of Leeds and east of Garforth at Micklefield, no. 297 *The Cottesmore* has a local train on 4th September 1945. The locomotive is travelling on the Leeds-Selby line, opened in 1834, with the NER building a spur from Micklefield to Church Fenton during the late 1860s removing the need to travel to South Milford to join the York & North Midland Railway line. Throughout the Second World War, no. 297 was stabled at Leeds Neville Hill shed.

Opposite above NO. 205 – HULL

A pair of D49s is pictured in Hull on 9th June 1935. The leading engine is no. 205 *The Albrighton*, whilst the one behind appears to be no. 251 *Derbyshire*. Approaching a year old at this time, no. 205 was new to Hull Botanic Gardens shed in July 1934 and remained there until May 1939 when moved on to York. No. 251 was still at Leeds Neville Hill, though just before the war also transferred, in this instance to Hull Botanic Gardens, beginning an association with the depot to last on and off to the late 1950s. Photograph courtesy Rail Photoprints.

Opposite below NO. 298 – HULL PARAGON STATION

No. 298 *The Pytchley* is at Hull Paragon station during the 1930s and appears to have been a recent visitor to works judging from the immaculate condition presented. New from Darlington in September 1933, the first general repair was carried out at the works nearly two years later from early May to late June 1935. The second took place following a further two-year period at which time a carriage heating connection was installed. Though recorded as unclassified repairs, no. 298 went on to have significant spells out of work at Darlington in 1938 and 1939.

Below NO. 359 – YORK

Standing at the south end of York station, with one of the two roundhouses there visible in the background, in the 1930s is no. 359 *The Fitzwilliam*. Darlington sent the locomotive to York when finished in September 1934 and this allocation lasted to early 1948. As one of the main depots in the North East, York had priority over locomotives and with the introduction of rotary cam D49s, the oscillating cam engines were transferred away. Just before no. 359 was built, York had ten D49s, with only one piston valve example. At the end of the decade, the LNER decided to focus certain types in specific places, though York's share of the class remained static.

Above NO. 365

Two 4-4-0s have teamed together to convey this mid-afternoon express on 31st July 1937. Piloting is no. 365 *The Morpeth* which was in service from December 1934 at Leeds Neville Hill. The train engine is Worsdell D20 Class 4-4-0 no. 1217. Amongst ten constructed at Gateshead in 1907, the locomotive's career lasted until September 1954. Originally classified R by the NER, a total of 60 were built starting 1899 at Gateshead and they were used on the company's main line expresses. After Grouping, the D20s were gradually displaced to secondary duties following the introduction of the Pacifics and the D49s. The first withdrawals were made in the early 1940s and was completed during 1957.

Above NO. 366 – HARROGATE STARBECK

No. 366 *The Oakley* is passing Harrogate Starbeck shed in 1936 and has a train consisting of tourist stock. Passenger traffic on the LNER amounted to just over a third of all receipts in the 1930s which was the lowest of the 'Big Four' main line companies. At the start of the decade, the collapse of heavy industry kept the company's finances in a precarious position, meaning the passenger market became particularly important. Some of the traffic had been recently lost to road transport, such as motorbuses, and the company looked to recoup receipts from excursions. Tourist stock was developed as a low-cost method of travel for this. Several 12-coach sets were ordered from York/Doncaster/Birmingham Railway Carriage & Wagon Co./Metropolitan Cammell. These were formed of two buffet carriages, four twin articulated open thirds and two open brake thirds. A departure from normal construction methods was the use of plywood side sheets to reduce costs, though interior supports continued to be teak. As with other coaches of this period, the interior was painted rather than varnished wood panels. The tourist trains proved popular and more sets were built in 1934, as well as 1938.

Below NO. 370 – NORTHALLERTON STATION

A Newcastle to Leeds train stands against the platform at Northallerton station behind no. 370 *The Rufford* in the 1930s. The line between York and Darlington reached the town in 1841 and the Leeds Northern Railway connected with Northallerton a decade later when the route between Leeds and Stockton opened. No. 370 was built in January 1935 and was first based from Neville Hill, then from early 1942 until the end of the decade was at Gateshead.

1946 NUMBERING

Above **NO. 2700 – DONCASTER STATION**

A local train is at Doncaster station behind the pioneer D49, no. 2700 *Yorkshire*. The locomotive has been renumbered as part of Edward Thompson's 1946 scheme and is also wearing black livery applied to all locomotives during the Second World War. 'LNER' on the tender has similarly been reduced to 'NE' as a money/materials/manpower saving measure.

Opposite above **NO. 374 – BRAMHOPE TUNNEL**

At the cost of 24 lives, Bramhope tunnel was excavated between Horsforth and Arthington starting 1845 and ending in 1849. At just over two miles long, the tunnel was part of the Leeds & Thirsk Railway, later Leeds Northern Railway line to Stockton. No. 374 *The Sinnington* is about to enter the northern portal, which has been awarded Grade II listed status, with a train for Leeds on 6th September 1945. The engine was Neville Hill-allocated from new in January 1935 to just after Nationalisation.

Opposite below **NO. 376**

The 75th and penultimate D49 was no. 376 *The Staintondale* which emerged from Darlington Works in February 1935. A few days later, the locomotive was followed by the final class member no. 377 *The Tynedale*. No. 376, which is perhaps at York shed in the late 1930s, reported for duty first at Leeds Neville Hill and remained there for 13 years.

Above NO. 2742 – GATESHEAD SHED

As mentioned, the LNER's policy of numbering was that of filling gaps in the stock list. When Edward Thompson became Chief Mechanical Engineer in 1941 following the death of Sir Nigel Gresley, he devised a complete renumbering scheme in priority of type. Express engines were to use the lowest numbers and shunters the highest. The D49s fell into the secondary passenger group and were allocated a block beginning no. 2700 and running to no. 2775. These were given to the engines in build order rather than numerical, whilst also meaning the eight piston valve D49s built in 1929 with numbers already in this range were renumbered 2728-2735. No. 2742 *The Braes of Derwent* was provided with the new number in October 1946 and is in the yard at Gateshead during June 1948, yet NE still adorns the tender. Well over a year would elapse before the BR number was applied and the locomotive had also moved on from Gateshead to York. Photograph courtesy Colour-Rail.

Opposite above NO. 2703

The partnership of the D49 with the Group Standard tender was broken for some of the class before the Second World War, as well as during the conflict and later. All of the locomotives were built new with the type, but of differing styles: stepped-out sides; straight sides. Just before the Second World War, the decision was made to remove the Group Standard tenders from the oscillating-cam engines and replace them with NER 4,125-gallon tenders with 5½-ton coal capacity. The reasoning behind this was the D49s did not require the facility of water pick-up apparatus, which was present on the Group Standard design, whereas new V2 Class 2-6-2s did. To save money a switch was proposed whereby the D49s acquired NER tenders from Q6 Class 0-8-0s and the V2 the Group Standard. Whilst the oscillating-cam locomotives were originally selected, piston valve no. 256 *Hertfordshire* and rotary cam no. 336 *The Quorn* also changed types, in November and August 1938 respectively. No. 256 became no. 2703 in January 1947 and has the tender here at an unidentified location around Nationalisation – note the LNER branding is still in full force on the tender and carriages, with the one behind no. 2703 a clerestory vehicle.

Opposite below NO. 2708 – BIRTLEY

South of Gateshead at Birtley, no. 2708 *Argyllshire* has a down freight on 20th August 1947. Around 10 days earlier, the locomotive had emerged from Darlington Works following a general repair, which was the first in two years and the last had taken place at Cowlairs. No. 270 had been removed from the locomotive in September 1946 and no. 2708 applied from this time until December 1949 when the British Railways number was used. *Argyllshire* has both the class designation and the shed allocation on the buffer beam, with Thornton Junction no. 2708's home from July 1943 until withdrawn.

Above NO. 2772 – FERRIBY STATION

Approx. seven miles from Hull, no. 2772 *The Sinnington* has a local train at Ferriby station around Nationalisation. The engine was renumbered from no. 374 in December 1946 and acquired the BR number in February 1949. At the latter date, an allocation to Harrogate Starbeck was a year old and lasted to the mid-1950s when a return to Leeds Neville Hill occurred briefly. Ferriby station was on the Hull & Selby Railway line and was opened in 1840. The number of running lines was later increased from two to four by the NER at the turn of the century. Photograph courtesy Rail-Online.

Opposite above NO. 2744 – COTTINGHAM

Approaching Cottingham with a local train in the mid-1940s is no. 2744 *The Cleveland*. The village was served by the Hull & Selby Railway from October 1846 and later the point for a junction which ran from the Bridlington branch line eastward to reach Hull Paragon station. No. 2744 is just north of Cottingham station and passing Northgate road level crossing which was controlled by Cottingham North signal box. The latter was subsequently removed and reassembled in Hull Streetlife transport museum (opened 1989). Photograph courtesy Rail-Online.

Opposite below NO. 2763 – LEEDS CITY STATION

After the Second World War, the LNER was keen to break the economy measures enforced on the company. Whilst a number of the express passenger engines were soon decorated in their colourful livery with LNER branding, the D49s had to remain content with plain black livery, though enjoyed the return of 'LNER' on the tenders to complement their new numbers. No. 2763 *The Fitzwilliam* lost no. 359 in November 1946 and perhaps received the lettering at a general repair in late summer 1947. A marked difference from the pre-war application was that for a number of classes shaded transfers were no longer used and both lettering and numbers were painted in yellow 12-in.-high characters and figures. Apparently ready to take water at Leeds City station in the late 1940s, no. 2763 has what is likely to be a local train. Photograph courtesy Rail-Online.

BRITISH RAILWAYS

Above NO. 62700 – LEEDS CITY STATION

Following Nationalisation of the railways in January 1948, several months elapsed before British Railways formulated policy for livery and numbering. With regard to the latter, the constituent companies had thousands added to the number in 1948, with ex-LNER locomotives allocated 60,000. The first D49, no. 2700 *Yorkshire* therefore received 62700 and this was used on the engine from April 1949. A feature particular to BR was the smokebox door numberplate but this continued to employ Gil Sans type of the LNER, whilst tenders first received 'British Railways' lettering, followed by an emblem, then grant of arms. *Yorkshire* is seen at Leeds City station on 9th September 1958 and was almost exactly a month away from withdrawal. The first D49 went to the scrapyard a year earlier. No. 62700 was employed at Hull Botanic Gardens from September 1957 until dismissed from service. Photograph by L. Rowe courtesy of Colour-Rail.

Opposite above and below NO. 62701 – DONCASTER

Just south of Doncaster station, two views of no. 62701 *Derbyshire* have been captured from St James's platform footbridge on 15th August 1959. The engine is engaged on empty stock movements between the station and the carriage sidings located amidst the two curves of Hexthorpe Junction where the East Coast Main Line connected with the Sheffield route. No. 62701 was also around a month away from being condemned when pictured and for the last three months Hull Dairycoates shed had a role for the locomotive. Both photographs by Geoff Warnes.

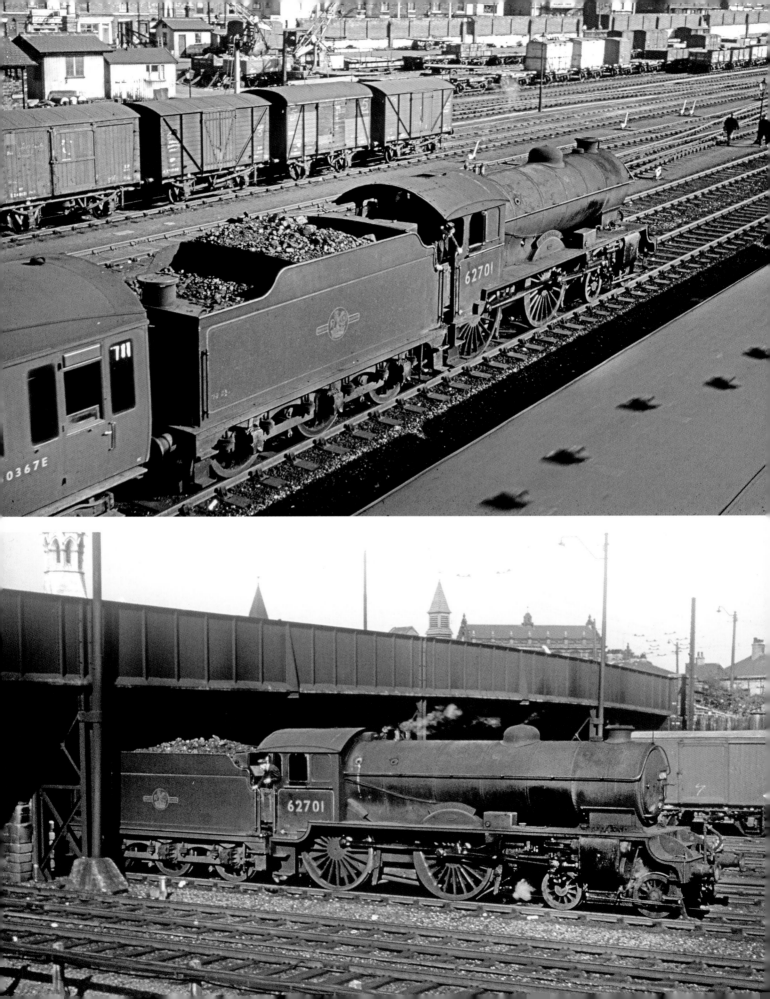

Above NO. 62704 – GLASGOW EASTFIELD SHED

Looking particularly work-worn outside Glasgow Eastfield shed in the late 1940s is no. 62704 *Stirlingshire*. Both types of D49s used a diagram 97 boiler and in some instances these crossed over between piston valve and rotary cam locomotives. This has been the case for no. 62704 and is identifiable from the square bracket on the boiler clothing plate above the mechanical lubricator which mounted the reversing gear for the rotary cam motion. The boiler was no. 126 and had been fitted in 1942 following use with no. 310 *Kinross-shire*. Though this was also a piston valve engine, the boiler originated with rotary cam locomotive no. 292 *The Southwold*. No. 62704 had travelled to Glasgow from Thornton Junction. Photograph courtesy Rail Photoprints.

Opposite above NO. 62702 – PILMOOR

South of Thirsk, Pilmoor was a sparsely inhabited area which became the location for two routes to join the East Coast Main Line. The Great North of England Railway originally built the line through the area, connecting York and Darlington in 1841. Later, a station was provided at Pilmoor during 1847 when the Pilmoor, Boroughbridge & Knaresborough Railway opened between Pilmoor and Boroughbridge. In the 1870s, this extended to Knaresborough to reach the East & West Yorkshire Junction line between Harrogate and York. The Thirsk and Malton route was laid by the York & North Midland Railway and joined the ECML just south of Pilmoor. This is the location for no. 62702 *Oxfordshire* which is hauling a stores train in the 1950s. Under the LNER, the section of the ECML south of Thirsk was upgraded to four tracks and this resulted in the reconstruction of Pilmoor station, as well as Pilmoor South signal box seen here. Photograph courtesy Rail-Online.

Opposite below NO. 62703 – SCARBOROUGH STATION

In the 1950s, no. 62703 *Hertfordshire* arrives at Scarborough station with a train from Leeds. The engine is still paired with a NER-style tender and this remained the case to withdrawal in June 1958. The first BR emblem is applied to the tender side, suggesting a date in the early to mid-1950s. During this period, no. 62703 was mainly stabled at Bridlington, though was at Hull Botanic Gardens for the last nine months in traffic. Photograph by T.G. Hepburn from Rail Archive Stephenson courtesy Rail-Online.

Above NO. 62705 – EDINBURGH HAYMARKET SHED

The British Railways mixed traffic black livery with white and red lining is partially visible under the grime carried by no. 62705 *Lanarkshire*. The locomotive is at Edinburgh Haymarket shed in 1958/59 when approaching the end, which occurred in November 1959. No. 62705 was based in Edinburgh from new, firstly at St Margaret's depot, then from March 1943 at Haymarket. Photograph by Bill Reed.

Opposite above NO. 62706 – EDINBURGH HAYMARKET SHED

No. 62706 *Forfarshire* stands in the yard at Edinburgh Haymarket shed during the late 1940s/early 1950s. With 'British Railways' on the tender, the locomotive also has BR's power classification on the cab side above the number. This was derived from practice on the London Midland & Scottish Railway whereby passenger and freight locomotives were graded with a number between 0 and 9 for their haulage capacity. The D49 Class was rated 4 with suffix 'P' for passenger duties. Also visible in the bottom-right corner is the route availability which was arranged under a system devised in the 1940s. The D49s had a particularly restricted route availability at RA8 which was one step below the Pacifics. Photograph courtesy Rail Photoprints.

Opposite below NO. 62707 – SCARBOROUGH STATION

A local train arrives at a relatively quiet Scarborough station behind no. 62707 *Lancashire* in the 1950s. From the middle of that decade, the locomotive was restless, moving between Bridlington and Hull to withdrawal in October 1959. Photograph courtesy Rail-Online.

Above NO. 62708 – DALMENY JUNCTION

Just south of the Forth Bridge, east and west spurs off the Edinburgh and Glasgow main line met in order to cross the Firth of Forth. This was done at Dalmeny and controlled by Dalmeny Junction signal box which stands here off to the left of no. 62708 *Argyllshire*. The locomotive is approaching with an Edinburgh to Dundee local train on 23rd July 1955. No. 62708 was working from Thornton Junction at this time and had been from July 1943. The engine was sent for scrap in May 1959. Photograph by David Anderson courtesy Rail Photoprints.

Opposite NO. 62709 – EDINBURGH HAYMARKET SHED

In January 1928, Darlington sent no. 277 *Berwickshire* into service at Edinburgh St Margaret's shed. Four years later, the engine moved to Perth and had a year there before returning to Edinburgh. During the Second World War, no. 277 arrived at Haymarket and remained to withdrawal in January 1960. The locomotive is 'on shed' there in the late 1950s as enginemen converse between duties. A non-standard feature on display here concerns the nameplate. Under both LNER and BR, the background colour was black, though there were exceptions, both official and unofficial. For instance, Gresley's A4s had a red background for certain class members, initially the 'Coronation' engines and then the 'silver' quartet, in addition to those named after officials of the company. No. 62709 (renumbered in September 1946 and December 1948) has a red background here which has likely stemmed from Haymarket shed's pride in presenting engines in the best condition possible: a similar position was taken by King's Cross depot, whilst others were content to run their charges into the ground. A blue backing to names was also seen under BR, as well as red and blue backgrounds to numberplates. Photograph by Bill Reed.

NO. 62711 – EDINBURGH ST MARGARET'S SHED

Though apparently out of service in April 1960, no. 62711 *Dumbartonshire* remained active until 1st May 1961. The engine was at Hawick for the last week in traffic, but is seen at Edinburgh St Margaret's shed here. Photograph by T.B. Owen courtesy of Colour-Rail.

Above NO. 62710 – BRIDLINGTON
An express is at Bridlington in the mid-1950s with no. 62710 *Lincolnshire*. The locomotive worked from the local shed for five months from September 1954 to January 1955. This was between spells at Hull Botanic Gardens. Photograph courtesy Rail-Online.

Below NO. 62712 – CARLISLE CANAL SHED
Condemned in July 1961, no. 62712 *Morayshire* was stored for several years before preserved. The locomotive is currently on the Bo'ness & Kinneil Railway under overhaul. Photograph by Gerald T. Robinson.

Above NO. 62712 – EDINBURGH DALRY ROAD SHED

In August 1962, no. 62712 *Morayshire* is being stored at Dalry Road shed, Edinburgh, following withdrawal a year earlier. For a brief period, the locomotive was used as a stationary boiler for a private company before returned to BR. After being moved on from Dalry Road, no. 62712 was stored at Dawsholm shed until taken for preservation. Dalry Road was a Caledonian Railway establishment absorbed by the London Midland & Scottish Railway at Grouping and examples of both companies' locomotives are in the yard here. Two CR McIntosh 3F Class 0-6-0s are seen, with no. 57654 and 57560 right and left in the distance respectively, a Stanier locomotive is behind no. 62712, as well as no. 57654, and BR Standard Class 4 2-6-0 no. 76105 is outside the shed building. Photograph by D.J. Dippie.

NO. 62712 – EDINBURGH DALRY ROAD SHED

A detail view taken of no. 62712 *Morayshire*'s nameplate at Dalry Road shed, Edinburgh in August 1962. Of note is the works plate situated on the splasher. This has been modified to take the locomotive's BR number in place of the first/ second LNER number. The latter was also retro-fitted to the plates following the 1946 scheme. Whilst Doncaster-built engines would have carried a works number, Darlington did not assign such an identifier until the 1950s. Photograph by D.J. Dippie.

Above NO. 62713 – EDINBURGH PRINCES STREET GARDENS

The line to the west out of Edinburgh Waverley station briefly appeared from a tunnel under the Mound into Princes Street Gardens before entering another tunnel to Haymarket. Building developments to the north of Edinburgh's Old Town in the early 18th century resulted in displaced earth which was deposited in Loch Nor sitting between the two settlements. This area was later landscaped into Princes Street Gardens and became the location for the Scottish National Gallery (out of view at the top right). The railways came to the area in the mid-1800s and the public gardens where several generations have viewed rail traffic moving in and out of Waverley station. In this instance, no. 62713 *Aberdeenshire* has been recorded with a local train on 27th April 1957. The locomotive was the first D49 withdrawal in September 1957 and left traffic after seven years at Thornton Junction depot. Prior to this, no. 62713 had been at Dundee from new in February 1928. Photograph courtesy Rail-Online.

Opposite above NO. 62714 – STIRLING SHED

Even though no. 62714 *Perthshire* appears to be paired with an ex-NER tender, this is in fact from an ex-Great Central Railway locomotive. Following the original switches made just before the Second World War, a second initiative was devised in the early 1940s owing to a shortage of materials. Thompson was rebuilding Q4 Class 0-8-0s as 0-8-0T locomotives for shunting duties leaving a number of spare tenders. At the same time, a number of new O2 Class 2-8-0s were being erected and these were provided with the Group Standard tenders from the early D49s. Most of the replacements were similar in appearance to the Group Standard, though had a smaller water capacity at 4,000 gallons. A few were provided with coal rails, but these were given sheet metal backings, making them look like the earlier NER tenders. No. 62714 switched types in June 1941 and remained coupled through to withdrawal in August 1959. The engine was a long-term servant at Stirling shed and is pictured there during the late 1950s. Photograph by Gerald T. Robinson.

Opposite below NO. 62715 – HAWICK SHED

At Hawick shed after working a local train is no. 62715 *Roxburghshire*. Seen in the late 1950s, the engine was condemned in late June 1959. During 31 years in traffic, no. 62715 was mainly at St Margaret's, apart from four years at Edinburgh Haymarket in the mid-1940s. Photograph by Bill Reed.

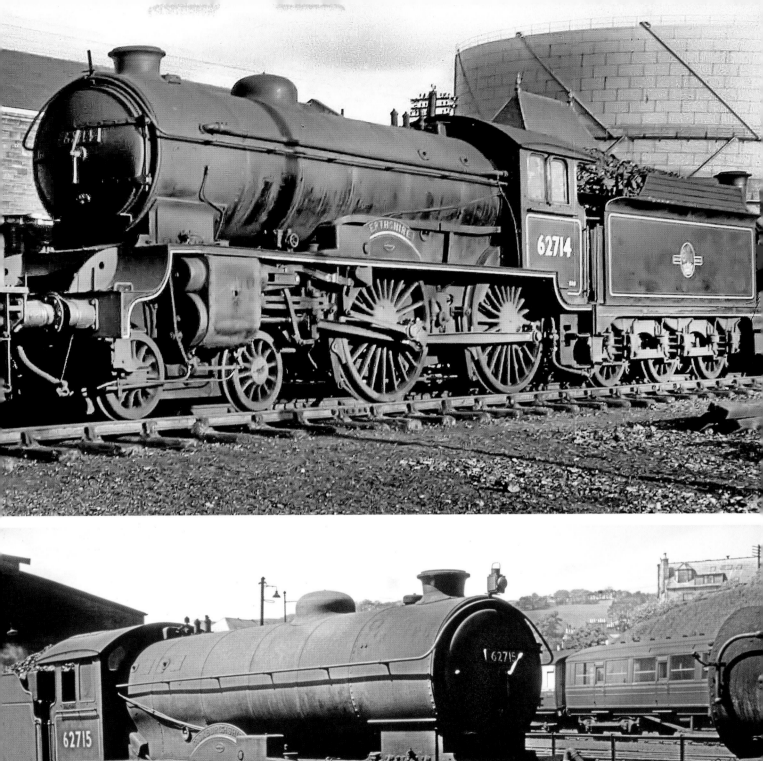

Above NO. 62716 – THORNTON JUNCTION SHED

With covering over the chimney (denoting a period of storage), no. 62716 *Kincardineshire* is at Thornton Junction shed in the late 1950s. The depot was one of the last in Scotland to receive a D49 engine, with no. 329 *Inverness-shire* arriving there just before the war. The number subsequently increased to around five for much of the 1950s, though in 1959 seven had congregated there. As Thornton Junction mainly served the Fife coalfield, few important passenger duties were to be undertaken and the class had to be content with local passenger and freight trains. Photograph by Bill Reed.

Opposite above NO. 62716 – DALMENY JUNCTION

A northbound local train passes Dalmeny Junction with no. 62716 *Kincardineshire* on 15th June 1957. The locomotive was coming to the end of 17 years at Thornton Junction at this time and in April 1960 had a year at St Margaret's before sent for scrap. Photograph by David Anderson courtesy Rail Photoprints.

Opposite below NO. 62715 – EDINBURGH WAVERLEY STATION

Standing by a platform at Edinburgh Waverley station during June 1958 is no. 62715 *Roxburghshire*. Like other piston valve engines, no. 62715 was given an ex-GCR tender in the early 1940s. Just after Nationalisation ten of these tenders were rebuilt with new tanks and coal spaces while reusing frames and wheels. The outward change of this modification was the tenders which resembled the second type of the Group Standard with straight sides. No. 62715 has such a tender here. Photograph by F. Hornby courtesy of Colour-Rail.

Above NO. 62718 – EDINBURGH ST MARGARET'S SHED

Simmering outside Edinburgh St Margaret's shed on 30th August 1960 is no. 62718 *Kinross-shire*. New in May 1928 as no. 310, the engine's first shed was Dundee and as a result tablet exchange equipment was necessary. This was retrospectively fitted at Cowlairs during the first month in service and likely removed when no. 62718 left the area in March 1952 to take employment at St Margaret's. *Kinross-shire* was renumbered in December 1946 and amongst a relatively small group of engines to use the 'E' prefix shortly after Nationalisation. The BR number was applied less than a year later. Photograph by Tony Cooke courtesy of Colour-Rail.

Opposite above NO. 62717 – DONCASTER STATION

On a damp and miserable day – 13th December 1958 – no. 62717 *Banffshire* waits to depart from Doncaster station's platform eight with a passenger train for Hull. The engine had been new to Dundee in March 1928 as no. 309 and remained in Scotland at several locations to early 1951. At this time, trials being conducted with the class saw a small number of rare inter-regional D49 transfers. No. 62717 was dispatched to Hull Botanic Gardens in place of no. 62743 *The Cleveland*. The engines remained in their respective regions to withdrawal, though no. 62717 was at Hull Dairycoates from June 1959 until condemned in January 1961. Photograph by Geoff Warnes.

Opposite below NO. 62717 – DARLINGTON SCRAPYARD

A grisly sight has been captured for posterity on 13th February 1961. Following official withdrawal exactly a month earlier, work is well underway cutting up no. 62717 *Banffshire* at Darlington scrapyard. Photograph by D.J. Dippie.

Below

NO. 62719 – EDINBURGH HAYMARKET SHED

As an early piston valve engine, no. 62719 *Peebles-shire* subsequently underwent several minor alterations. The cylinder drain pipes were originally much shorter and have changed to the longer versions, though the linkage for the drain cocks remains in front of the cylinders, whereas the rotary cam locomotives had this placed behind. No. 62719 was also without front footsteps when new (as no. 311) and these have been added, whilst sanding for the driving wheels in forward motion only was provided. Soon after arriving at St Margaret's when new from Darlington the engine was amongst a number of Scottish engines provided with rearward sanding as well. A tender change is also part of *Peebles-shire*'s history and an ex-GCR tender was coupled from February 1942 until condemned in January 1960. The locomotive is at Edinburgh Haymarket shed on 26th August 1958. Photograph by D.J. Dippie.

Above NO. 62718 – DALMENY STATION

The Firth of Forth was crossed using boats before the advent of the Forth Bridge in 1890. Some 25 years before this, the North British Railway completed a short branch from the Edinburgh-Glasgow line to South Queensferry for the transport of passengers and freight to the crossing. This line was later extended to Port Edgar. Dalmeny station was one of several on the route and first opened in 1866. A second facility followed on the completion of the Forth Bridge, opening at the same time. The station continues to serve passengers for Glasgow, Edinburgh, the North and local area. No. 62718 *Kinross-shire* is viewed passing through Dalmeny station with a southbound train from Dundee to Edinburgh Waverley on 23rd July 1955. Photograph by David Anderson courtesy Rail Photoprints.

Opposite and above NO. 62719 EDINBURGH HAYMARKET SHED

Two views of no. 62719 *Peebles-shire* on home ground at Edinburgh Haymarket shed. Above, the locomotive is on the turntable, with a Stanier Class 5 lurking in the background, on 11th April 1957, whilst left, no. 62719 rests during the late 1950s. In common with shed mate no. 62709, *Peebles-shire* has the non-standard red background to the nameplate. Also similarly, the two had transferred from St Margaret's to Haymarket in March 1943 and were used by the depot to the late 1950s. No. 62719 was briefly at Hawick before condemned at the start of 1960. Both photographs by Bill Reed.

Above NO. 62720 – SEAMER

Another variation in tender is visible here behind no. 62720 *Cambridgeshire*, which is at Seamer – south of Scarborough – in the 1950s. The engine was the recipient of an ex-NER tender in March 1938 and this had cut-back coal rails, whereas the others had rails which curved down at the ends. The pairing lasted for a number of years and was distinctive for no. 62720. With a local train, *Cambridgeshire* was a long-term servant at Hull Botanic Gardens and had left Scarborough for there in June 1943. Photograph by P.J. Hughes courtesy of Colour-Rail.

Opposite above NO. 62722 – SCARBOROUGH STATION

No. 62722 *Huntingdonshire* is light engine at Scarborough station on 13th December 1958. The locomotive was one of two D49s experimentally fitted with the 'Kylchap' blastpipe and chimney which was developed by Kyösti Kylälä and André Chapelon. This device aimed to reduce back pressure at the cylinders and improve the draught through the firebox, boiler and smokebox with the result of better combustion. As fitted to the D49, no particular benefits were obtained, yet Gresley persisted with the apparatus on other types, particularly the A4 Pacifics, and achieved operation closer to that demonstrated by Chapelon in France. No. 62722 (as no. 322) was equipped with the chimney from April 1929 to September 1930. At the latter date, the locomotive also reverted to the standard Gresley '2 to 1' lever arrangement. *Huntingdonshire* was at Leeds Neville Hill for the trials and soon after their conclusion transferred to Hull Botanic Gardens. Photograph courtesy Colour-Rail.

Opposite below NO. 62722 – YORK SHED

On 13th April 1957, no. 62722 *Huntingdonshire* is between duties at York shed, with a Gresley V2 adjacent. The locomotive moved from Botanic Gardens to Dairycoates in June 1959 and was condemned there in October. Darlington scrapped no. 62722 subsequently. Photograph by Bill Reed.

Above NO. 62723 – DARLINGTON SCRAPYARD
Standing behind an almost completely dismantled Thompson L1 Class 2-6-4T – no. 67711 – is no. 62723 *Nottinghamshire*. Seen on 13th February 1961, the task has begun on cutting-up the D49 which was withdrawn from Hull Dairycoates a month earlier. The locomotive had been there 18 months, following a transfer from Botanic Gardens. Photograph by D.J. Dippie.

Opposite above NO. 62723 – DONCASTER STATION
In the mid-1920s, Leeds, Bradford and Harrogate received a dedicated Pullman car train to/from King's Cross. A decade later, travellers from Hull were offered a connection to the train, joining the main body at Doncaster. At the same time, the name changed from the 'West Riding Pullman', to the 'Yorkshire Pullman', recognising the new scope of the service. With the introduction of the 'West Riding Limited' streamline train in 1937, the LNER decided to concentrate the Leeds/ Bradford traffic on their own service and the 'Yorkshire Pullman' ran via York to Harrogate, still offering the Hull connection. All named trains ceased during the war and the 'Yorkshire Pullman' returned on 4th November 1946, though now a Leeds/ Bradford service again after the disbanding of the 'West Riding Limited' set. The timings in the 1950s were 10.07 departure from Harrogate to reach Doncaster where the 10.30 from Hull was connected to continue southward at 11.50. Arrival in the capital was scheduled at 14.38. Twelve coaches formed the complete train, with four of these from Hull: second-class brake; first-class kitchen; first-class parlour; second-class kitchen. From Doncaster, the train was usually handled by Peppercorn A1 Class Pacifics, whilst on the other routes a selection of motive power was employed, including D49s from Hull. One engaged for the task on 16th July 1960 is no. 62723 *Nottinghamshire* which is in a particularly unpresentable condition given the prestige of the service. No. 62723 was in service for another six months then sent for scrap. Photograph by David P. Williams courtesy Rail-Online.

Opposite below NO. 62723 – DARLINGTON SCRAPYARD
A detail of no. 62723's nameplate taken whilst in the scrapyard at Darlington on 13th February 1961. Whilst the works plate has been removed, the nameplate remains in place and would have proved a particular prize for a collector. Interestingly, a works plate from the locomotive has been to auction. Photograph by D.J. Dippie.

Above **NO. 62726 – LEEDS CITY STATION**

An eastbound express for Hull departs from Leeds City station in the 1950s with no. 62726 *The Meynell*. Just after Nationalisation the locomotive moved from Harrogate to York and had five years at the latter before transferring to Scarborough. No. 62726 was another early withdrawal at the end of 1957. Photograph by Kenneth Field from Rail Archive Stephenson courtesy Rail-Online.

Opposite above **NO. 62724 – DONCASTER STATION**

No. 62724 *Bedfordshire* was built at Darlington as no. 335 in August 1928. At this time, the locomotive was fitted with oscillating cam valve gear, though by November 1938 piston valves had been provided. A unique feature to no. 335 when new was a multiple valve regulator which operated in the superheater section of the boiler instead of the live steam part. This offered the advantage of increasing the lifespan of the superheater elements, whilst five valves in the superheater header offered an improved control over the steam allowed to the cylinders. Whilst satisfactory, and the extension of the scheme to V2 and Peppercorn A2 locomotives, no. 335 saw the equipment removed in August 1943. In November 1938, the engine had lost the original tender and received an NER replacement, whilst this was also changed to a GCR type in December 1953. *Bedfordshire* arrives at Doncaster station from the north during the 1950s. The locomotive was another early withdrawal at the end of 1957. Photograph by P.J. Hughes courtesy of Colour-Rail.

Opposite below **NO. 62725 – EDINBURGH HAYMARKET SHED**

One of two D49s sent to Stirling in the early 1950s was no. 62725 *Inverness-shire*. The engine arrived at the ex-North British Railway shed in October 1953, only to move on to the ex-Caledonian Railway facility in early 1956 before the closure of the engine's former home in late 1957. No. 62725 was mainly used on passenger trains from Stirling to Edinburgh Princes Street and is seen at Haymarket depot for servicing on 28th August 1956. Photograph by D.J. Dippie.

Above NO. 62727 – DARLINGTON SCRAPYARD
On 13th February 1961, no. 62727 *The Quorn* is still relatively intact at Darlington scrapyard, though the fox and works plate have been removed. Withdrawal occurred a month earlier, as was the case for Raven B16 Class 4-6-0 no. 61446 which is adjacent. Just visible in the background is another D49 – no. 62763 *The Fitzwilliam*. Photograph by D.J. Dippie.

Opposite above NO. 62727 – HARROGATE STATION
A Liverpool to Newcastle cross-country express has been caught at Harrogate station with no. 62727 *The Quorn* on 29th November 1951. From pre-Grouping days, this train was important for connecting the two ports and several ran daily. Under BR, these took a number of routes, including via York and from Leeds to Harrogate which was the quickest route. Photograph courtesy *Yorkshire Post Newspapers*.

Opposite below NO. 62727 – SCARBOROUGH SHED
South of Scarborough station, a large engine shed was present on the west side of the line, with a brick works located to both the east and west. No. 62727 rests outside the depot, which suffered from subsidence problems resulting in the sturdy-looking supports holding the gable ends up. Seen on 21st June 1959, *The Quorn* was three months away from a move between Harrogate and Hull Dairycoates. Photograph by K.C.H. Fairey courtesy of Colour-Rail.

Above NO. 62728 – DARLINGTON WORKS

No. 62728 *Cheshire* was sent from Thornton Junction to Darlington Works for repair in late October 1959. The engine sits amongst a number of others hoping for admittance on 26th October 1959, yet *Cheshire* was condemned three days later following 30 years of service for both the LNER and BR. Photograph by Bill Reed.

Opposite NO. 62728 – THORNTON JUNCTION SHED

In the late 1950s, no. 62728 *Cheshire* has been pictured out of service at Thornton Junction shed. The locomotive was allocated there between February 1957 and October 1959. An ex-GCR tender was used by no. 62728 from 1942 and appears to be one of the rebuilt ones with straight sides here. Photograph by Bill Reed.

Above NO. 62729 – EDINBURGH HAYMARKET SHED

Thornton Junction's no. 62729 *Rutlandshire* visits Edinburgh Haymarket shed for servicing on 11th April 1957. The locomotive had previously worked from the last mentioned between July 1929 and December 1933. At the latter date, *Rutlandshire* became one of four D49s stationed at Carlisle for Edinburgh and Newcastle duties. Just before Nationalisation, a transfer to Thornton Junction occurred and this lasted through the 1950s. Photograph by Bill Reed.

Opposite NO. 62729 – EDINBURGH ST MARGARET'S SHED

Undergoing firebox cleaning at Edinburgh St Margaret's shed around 1960 is no. 62729 *Rutlandshire*. The locomotive was originally numbered 2754 and became no. 2729 in July 1946, with the BR number applied from September 1948. The engine's final allocation was to St Margaret's depot in April 1960 and lasted until condemned in May 1961. Photograph by Gerald T. Robinson.

Above NO. 62732 – CARLISLE CANAL SHED

No. 62732 *Dumfries-shire* rests at Carlisle Canal shed in June 1953. The locomotive was another late 1930s transfer, in this instance from Glasgow Eastfield to Carlisle, but remained there longer than no. 62729 by around three years. The engine was in Yorkshire briefly at Harrogate and York before moving back to Carlisle and remained until withdrawn in November 1958. Photograph by John Hilmer courtesy of Colour-Rail.

Opposite NO. 62731 – GILLING STATION

On 23rd June 1957, the Railway Correspondence & Travel Society's branches in the North East and Sheffield came together for an excursion named the 'Yorkshire Coast Rail Tour'. This began in Leeds behind Worsdell D20 Class 4-4-0 no. 62387, which lasted just a few months more afterwards, and travelled eastward to York. There, no. 62731 *Selkirkshire* was engaged to take the party forward to Alne where Worsdell J71 0-6-0T no. 68246 ran along the Easingwold Railway with the passengers who were conveyed in open wagons. On the return to Alne, no. 62731 took the train forward to Kirby Moorside before going back to Gilling and using the line via Driffield and Flamborough to reach Scarborough, then Whitby. For the return, *Selkirkshire* went on the route through Goathland, Pickering and Malton to York before going on to Leeds. No. 62731 pauses with the tour here at Gilling station. Photograph by P.J. Hughes courtesy of Colour-Rail.

Below

NO. 62733 – THORNTON JUNCTION SHED

A broadside view of no. 62733 *Northumberland* on 23rd August 1958 as the engine is turned at Thornton Junction shed. The village of Thornton (north of Kirkcaldy) was provided with a station in the September following the opening of the Edinburgh & Northern Railway in July 1848. At the aforementioned date, a locomotive shed was built and the facilities were later upgraded by the NBR to a four-track depot in 1896. These were in use to the 1930s when the LNER demolished the depot and erected a new six-track shed on the branch to Dunfermline, west of Thornton Junction. A repair shop was included, along with a mechanical coaling plant and 70 ft turntable. The shed was closed in April 1967 and later demolished. Photograph by K.C.H. Fairey courtesy of Colour-Rail.

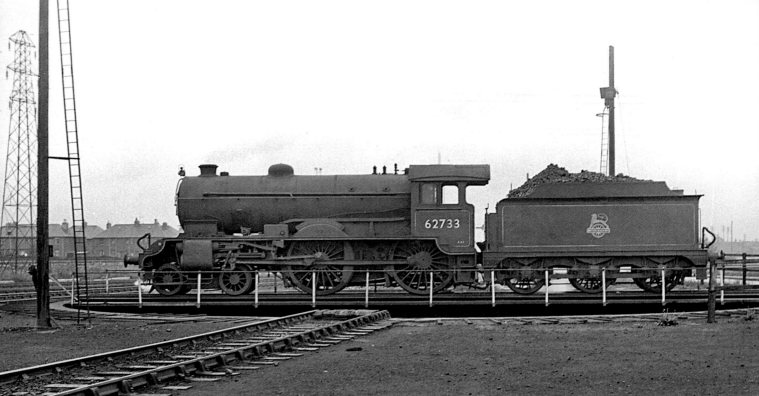

Above **NO. 62733 – JAMESTOWN VIADUCT**

On the north bank of the Firth of Forth, the line between North Queensferry and Inverkeithing crossed the land near the village of Jamestown on a viaduct. This opened at the same time as the Forth Bridge in 1890 and had four spans, each over 100 ft long. No. 62733 *Northumberland* is southbound near the viaduct and heading to the Forth Bridge with a local train from Dundee to Edinburgh on 26th March 1956. Photograph by David Anderson courtesy Rail Photoprints.

Below NO. 62733 – CARLISLE STATION

On the through lines at Carlisle station on 1st April 1961, no. 62733 *Northumberland* was around three weeks away from withdrawal following thirty-two years in traffic. Darlington works later scrapped the engine. Photograph by D. Forsyth courtesy of Colour-Rail.

Above NO. 62733 – EDINBURGH HAYMARKET

A local train to Dundee passes Edinburgh Haymarket shed, which is visible in the background on the left, in 1955 behind no. 62733 *Northumberland*. The locomotive was originally allocated to Glasgow Eastfield when new from Darlington in March 1929, though transferred to St Margaret's three months later. In early 1933, the engine, as LNER no. 2758, returned to Eastfield and was there for ten years until a move to Haymarket occurred. This allocation was still running when no. 62733 was pictured and ended in early 1958 when Thornton Junction received the locomotive. Photograph by David Anderson courtesy Rail Photoprints.

Above NO. 62734 – CARLISLE CANAL SHED

On 16th August 1960, no. 62734 *Cumberland* is again out of service (see opposite) at Carlisle Canal shed. Most depots, especially larger ones such as Carlisle Canal, had lines of locomotives in storage as traffic requirements often varied leaving some out of work. Towards the end of steam, the introduction of diesels and DMUs for local trains also contributed to steam engines being placed in the storage lines. No. 62734 was based at Carlisle from July 1951 and was condemned there in March 1961. Photograph by Gerald T. Robinson.

Opposite NO. 62734 – CARLISLE CANAL SHED

Being a piston valve engine, no. 62734 *Cumberland* was part of the tender swaps carried out in the early 1940s. The locomotive was equipped with a GC-type tender at this time, though in September 1947 a switch occurred – likely with no. 62727 *Buckinghamshire* – and no. 62734 returned to traffic from a general repair with an NE-type tender. This was paired with the engine through to withdrawal. At Carlisle Canal shed on 15th May 1959, the locomotive is in storage and awaiting a return to duties. Photograph by Bill Reed.

Above NO. 62735 – SCARBOROUGH

Leaving Scarborough station, with what is likely a York-bound express, is no. 62735 *Westmorland*. The last of the piston valve class members built, as LNER no. 2760 the locomotive was in traffic for June 1929 and like other engines from this batch was new to Scotland at Glasgow Eastfield. A feature of earlier engines delivered to the area was steam reversing gear which proved unpopular. For the piston valve engines (nos 2753-2760) this reverted to standard screw reverse. This group also had steam brakes from new and Diamond soot blowers, which were used to keep the boiler tubes free from detritus. No. 62735 left Scotland for Carlisle in December 1946 and from September 1950 was in Yorkshire. First at Harrogate, then York and finally Scarborough in April 1954. Withdrawal occurred in August 1958. Photograph courtesy Rail-Online.

Below NO. 62736 – HARROGATE STATION

Harrogate was first served by the York & North Midland Railway which laid a line from Church Fenton. A station was opened by the company in July 1848, whilst another facility – Starbeck – appeared nearby later in the year as the Leeds Northern Railway passed by on the way to Thirsk. When the companies became part of the NER a new station was built on the present site and a connection made between the two lines. At the station on 29th November 1951 is no. 62736 *The Bramham Moor* which has a northbound local train. Also prominent is Harrogate North signal box opened by the LNER. This continues to stand and control movements in the area, despite the reconstruction of the station taking place in the mid-1960s. Photograph courtesy *Yorkshire Post Newspapers*.

Below NO. 62737

In May 1932 LNER no. 211 *The York and Ainsty* was completed at Darlington and was one of several equipped new with Goodall articulated drawbars. These offered buffering between the engine and tender. During the early 1940s these were removed from those locomotives fitted and no. 211 was affected following a general repair completed in November 1941. At this time the engine was allocated to Tweedmouth, having started work at Neville Hill, later moving to Gateshead in 1934. In May 1946 *The York and Ainsty*'s final allocation began and this was to Hull Botanic Gardens, which could be the location for this image captured around the mid-1950s. Photograph by D. Preston courtesy of Colour-Rail.

Above NO. 62738 – ARTHINGTON

Arthington station was opened by the Leeds & Thirsk Railway in 1849 as Pool, though the facility had to be resited when the Otley & Ilkley Joint line was opened by the NER and Midland Railway in 1865. A junction between the two routes was made both north and south of Arthington station (Pool was renamed in 1852), with the north junction and signal box being seen here with no. 62738 *The Zetland* in February 1958. The engine was Harrogate-allocated at the time. Photograph courtesy *Yorkshire Post Newspapers*.

NO. 62738 – HARROGATE STARBECK SHED

In storage at Harrogate Starbeck shed in the late 1950s is no. 62738 *The Zetland.* Photograph by Bill Reed.

Above NO. 62738 – HARROGATE STARBECK SHED

Particularly well-presented, no. 62738 *The Zetland* is at Harrogate shed in 1953. In September 1948 the engine was allocated to the depot and this was the case to September 1959. Photograph courtesy Rail Photoprints.

Below NO. 62738 – DARLINGTON SCRAPYARD

Leaving Harrogate in September 1959, no. 62738 was briefly at York before sent for scrap at Darlington. The end approaches for the locomotive here on 26th October 1959. Photograph by D.J. Dippie.

Opposite and above **NO. 62739 – SCARBOROUGH LONDESBOROUGH ROAD STATION**
In the late 19th and early 20th centuries, holiday traffic to coastal resorts was particularly intense. This was the case at Scarborough which necessitated the construction of a relief station just to the south of the terminus as space was lacking there. Opened in 1908, the new station was named Washbeck and operated as required, being out of the public timetable until 1933. At this time, the name was changed to Londesborough Road station and remained so until closure in late August 1963. No. 62739 *The Badsworth* is at the station in these two views taken in August 1960. The locomotive worked at the local shed but was soon to be condemned in October. Both photographs by Bill Reed.

NO. 62739 – SCARBOROUGH STATION

On 23rd August 1956, no. 62739 *The Badsworth* waits to take this train to a platform at Scarborough station. An ex-NER tender is coupled to the engine and had been from November 1955. The pairing lasted to May 1958. Photograph by George C. Lander courtesy Rail Photoprints.

Above NO. 62739
During the mid- to late 1950s, no. 62739 *The Badsworth* has an express. Photograph by P.J. Hughes courtesy of Colour-Rail.

Below NO. 62739 – SCARBOROUGH STATION
Leaving Scarborough station with an express in 1954 is no. 62739 *The Badsworth*. Photograph from the John Day Collection courtesy Rail Photoprints.

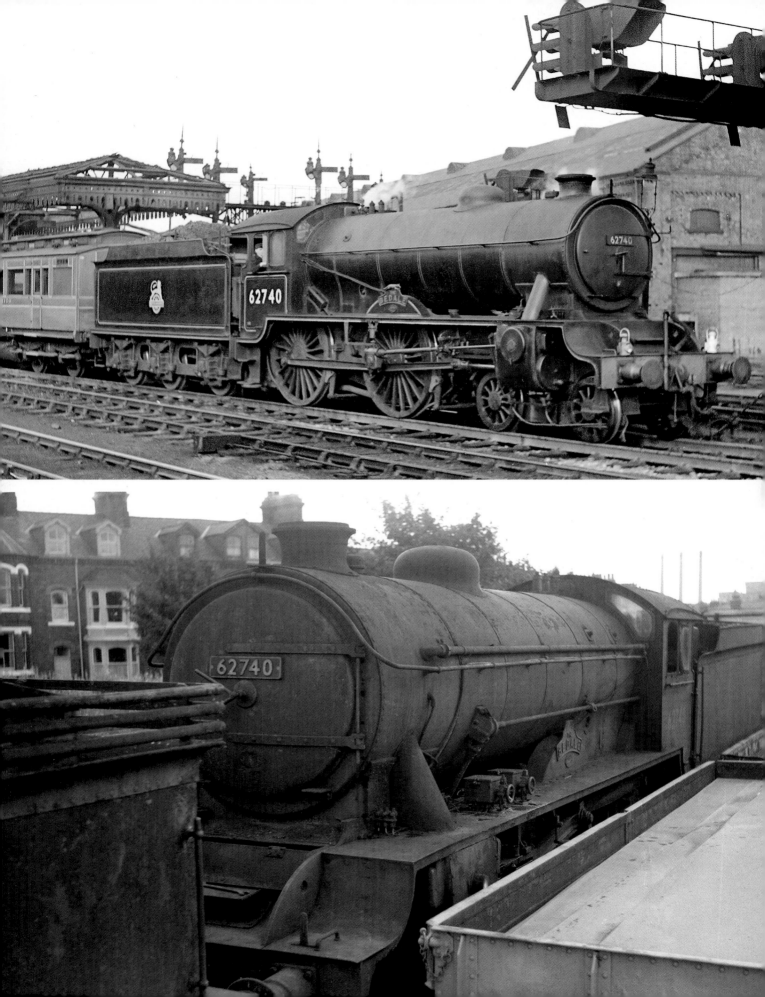

Above NO. 62741 – HULL BOTANIC GARDENS SHED

The D49s developed a reputation for uncomfortable riding for engine crews which persisted for some time. In an effort to address the issue, British Railways selected five to use steel axleboxes and a redesigned front bogie. No. 62741 *The Blankney* was the first to be modified in August 1949. As a result of the change, a third mechanical lubricator was fitted to the running plate and is present here. Between duties in the yard at Hull Botanic Gardens shed on 26th August 1958, the locomotive has Gresley V3 Class 2-6-2T no. 67684 standing behind. Photograph by K.C.H. Fairey courtesy of Colour-Rail.

Opposite above NO. 62740 – YORK STATION

No. 62740 *The Bedale* is at York station in 1950 with the ex-North Eastern Railway inspection saloon. This was constructed in the early 1870s as a third-class carriage and converted later in the decade for use by the company's officers. The saloon was rebuilt again at the turn of the century and went on to serve until the late 1960s when purchased privately for preservation. No. 62740 was fresh from a general repair and acquired the BR number at this time. Photograph courtesy Rail Photoprints.

Opposite below NO. 62740 – DARLINGTON SCRAPYARD

On 10th September 1960 – six weeks after condemned – no. 62740 *The Bedale* waits in the scrapyard at Darlington. As mentioned, lubrication was an afterthought when the class was introduced. The rotary cam engines received two Wakefield 8-feed lubricators – seen here on the running plate – from new to supply the valves and cylinders. The axleboxes received oil from inside the cab. Whilst name and works plates are still in place, the cast-metal fox has been removed. Photograph by D.J. Dippie.

Below

NO. 62743 – EDINBURGH HAYMARKET

No. 62743 *The Cleveland* was another D49 equipped with steel axleboxes and redesigned bogie under BR. These items were fitted in December 1950 and as a result was transferred to Scotland from Hull. In early 1951 no. 62743 was taken on at Edinburgh Haymarket and is opposite the running shed here in the late 1950s. The locomotive survived to May 1960. Photograph by Bill Reed.

Above **NO. 62742 – LEEDS CITY STATION**

Leeds Central – opened off Wellington Street in 1854 – was the meeting point for several railway companies which reached the town, later city. The railways concerned were the London & North Western, Lancashire & Yorkshire, North Eastern and Great Northern. Yet, the station was soon found to be too cramped and the LNWR and NER companies moved to Leeds New (later Leeds City) station. This station was still off Wellington Street, but had improved connections to the companies' lines. Leeds New station was built over the River Aire and opened for traffic in 1869. After Grouping, the Midland Railway's Leeds Wellington station, sited adjacently, also came under the ownership of the London Midland & Scottish Railway, with the jointly owned Leeds New. In 1938 work was carried out to join the two structures creating Leeds City station, which is still in use today. No. 62742 *The Braes of Derwent* is departing there in the 1950s with a train for Hull. Photograph by Kenneth Field from Rail Archive Stephenson courtesy Rail-Online.

Opposite and above NO. 62743 – EDINBURGH HAYMARKET SHED

Two scenes featuring no. 62743 *The Cleveland* at Edinburgh Haymarket shed in the late 1950s (left) and on 11th April 1957. When the first D49s with rotary cam valve gear were introduced, the cams were restricted to five cut-off positions. This was soon found to be disadvantageous to the economical working of the locomotives and a camshaft which allowed fine selection of cut-off was fitted to no. 282 *The Hurworth*. At the first general repair this was removed and replaced by a new camshaft with seven positions for cut-off. As LNER no. 269, *The Cleveland* was the second class member fitted in June 1934. Also of interest is the red number plate and red background to the nameplate. Both Photographs by Bill Reed.

NO. 62744 – LEEDS NEVILLE HILL SHED
On 27th November 1951, no. 62744 *The Holderness* is at Neville Hill shed, Leeds. Photograph courtesy *Yorkshire Post Newspapers*.

Above NO. 62744 – DUNDEE WEST SHED
Using the turntable at Dundee West shed on 20th September 1955 is no. 62744 *The Holderness*. In 1951, the engine received the axlebox modification and in early 1952 transferred to Dundee. Photograph by Bill Reed.

Below NO. 62744 – THORNTON JUNCTION SHED
No. 62744 *The Holderness* is stored out of service at Thornton Junction shed in the late 1950s. Photograph by Bill Reed.

Above NO. 62745 – LEEDS

An express approaches Leeds with no. 62745 *The Hurworth* on 20th April 1951. At this time, the locomotive was York-based and this allocation covered the period November 1948 to December 1954. No. 62745 had been new to Leeds Neville Hill as LNER no. 282 in October 1932, though this proved to be brief as Hull took the services of the engine in May 1933. *The Hurworth* was the class member to take part in the trial with the new camshaft design and was the first to receive the seven-step cut-off. Photograph courtesy *Yorkshire Post Newspapers*.

Below NO. 62747 – YORK STATION

As the piston valve D49s had cylinders cast as one unit the steam passages were internal, whereas the poppet valve engines had external steam pipes, creating a further difference between the two types. Early in 1958, no. 62747 *The Percy* had the cylinders replaced. The engine stands with an express at York station during mid-October. No. 62747 was based locally at this time but in the following month a transfer to Carlisle occurred and saw the locomotive to withdrawal in March 1961. Photograph by D.J. Dippie.

NO. 62747 – CARLISLE CANAL SHED

On the storage line at Carlisle Canal shed during mid-May 1959 is no. 62747 *The Percy*, as well as class mate no. 62734 *Cumberland*. Photograph by Bill Reed.

Above NO. 62749 – LEEDS HOLBECK LOW LEVEL STATION

A London St Pancras to Bradford train travels through Holbeck Low Level station, Leeds, on 22nd November 1951. At the head is no. 62749 *The Cottesmore*. Photograph courtesy *Yorkshire Post Newspapers*.

Below NO. 62748 – YORK STATION

A local service approaches the south end of York station with no. 62748 *The Southwold* during 1954. Photograph from the John Day Collection courtesy Rail Photoprints.

Above NO. 62749 – HARROGATE STATION

No. 62749 *The Cottesmore* is slightly unusual in having the BR number applied to the buffer beam rather than on a smokebox numberplate. Holes and bolts are present in the normal position below the top hinge strap. The BR number was first carried in April 1948, replacing the second LNER number (used from July 1946), whilst the original number was 297 when constructed at Darlington in August 1933. No. 62749 approaches Harrogate station here with a train of empty stock on 29th November 1951. Working from Starbeck shed at this time, a move to Neville Hill took place in 1955. Photograph courtesy *Yorkshire Post Newspapers*.

Opposite above NO. 62750 – HULL DAIRYCOATES SHED

No. 62750 *The Pytchley* had yet to start an association with a Hull shed, despite being in Dairycoates yard in 1951. Allocated to Bridlington, the locomotive went on to work from Hull for most of 1955 and returned again in September 1957 for just over a year before condemned. Of note is the plain tender (no emblem, lettering or lining) and the departmental tender standing behind. Photograph courtesy Rail-Online.

Opposite below NO. 62751 – YORK STATION

On 7th September 1958, no. 62751 *The Albrighton* is at York station. An ex-NER tender was attached to the engine in 1953 and used until condemned in March 1959. Photograph courtesy Rail-Online.

Below
NO. 62752 – LEEDS NEVILLE HILL SHED

When all the D49s were in service, Leeds Neville Hill shed accumulated around ten class members and this remained relatively static until the late 1940s. At this time, Thompson's B1 Class 4-6-0 was introduced and fared better with the heavier loads then prevailing. This led to the number at Leeds diminishing by around half as engines moved elsewhere to replace older, life-expired classes. No. 62752 *The Atherstone* provides an example of this as the engine left Neville Hill for Harrogate in October 1947. In the yard at Leeds on 27th November 1951, no. 62752 still has a presentable appearance despite being almost six months from the last general repair. During this event, the ex-NER tender – carried from April 1949 – was replaced by a Group Standard tender. The locomotive was in service until July 1958. Photograph courtesy *Yorkshire Post Newspapers*.

Above NO. 62753 – ARTHINGTON

A short distance to the north of Arthington, no. 62753 *The Belvoir* has a relief express for Liverpool in July 1958. A change of tender type occurred in July 1952 as an ex-NER type was paired, but under a year later a Group Standard tender was coupled. Photograph courtesy *Yorkshire Post Newspapers*.

Above NO. 62754 – DONCASTER STATION

A crowded scene captured at the south end of Doncaster station, c. 1950. No. 62754 *The Berkeley* features and possibly has an officers' special train, whilst Gresley B17 Class no. 61660 *Hull City* is light engine on the left. Though the latter was named after the football team based in the city, the locomotive did not have an association with the place and was March-allocated at the time. The B17s worked in East Anglia and on the ex-Great Central Railway main line making visits to the East Coast port unlikely. No. 62754 had a brief spell in Hull under the LNER, taking a berth at Botanic Gardens from November 1934 until July 1935. The engine returned there in October 1945 and remained until condemned in November 1958. Both no. 62754 and no. 61660 have received the BR number and company lettering on the tender. Photograph by Geoff Warnes.

Opposite above NO. 62753 AND NO. 62700 – LEEDS CITY STATION

Two D49s are set to leave Leeds City station with local trains on 9th September 1958. On the left, no. 62753 *The Belvoir* has the 17.30 service to Harrogate, whilst on the next platform is no. 62700 *Yorkshire* with a Selby train, due to leave slightly earlier at 17.13. Photograph by L. Rowe courtesy of Colour-Rail.

Opposite below NO. 62753 – HARROGATE STARBECK SHED

No. 62753 was another class member displaced from Leeds Neville Hill to Harrogate following the introduction of Thompson B1s after the war. New to Leeds as LNER no. 217 in July 1934, the aforementioned move took place just before Nationalisation in October 1947. By this time the engine had been renumbered to no. 2753 and BR's identification was displayed from April 1948. *The Belvoir* has been pictured here in the yard at Harrogate Starbeck during 1958. A brief transfer to York was apparently made in September 1959 before condemned later in the month. Photograph courtesy Rail Photoprints.

NO. 62753 – HARROGATE STATION
A Liverpool to Newcastle express has reached
Harrogate station on 29th November 1951.
No. 62753 *The Belvoir* is piloting Thompson B1
no. 61069. Photograph courtesy *Yorkshire Post
Newspapers.*

Above NO. 62754 – DARLINGTON SCRAPYARD
The torch gang makes a start on no. 62754 *The Berkeley* on 29th July 1959. Photograph by David P. Williams courtesy Rail-Online.

Below NO. 62755 – YORK
Whilst working an express freight, Gresley A4 no. 60019 *Bittern* is held by a signal near York, c. 1950, as no. 62755 *The Bilsdale* passes with a local train. Photograph courtesy Rail Photoprints.

Opposite and above NO. 62755 – LEEDS CITY STATION

The two images here show no. 62755 *The Bilsdale* at Leeds City station on 8th October 1951. The driver is evidently taking pride in the appearance of his engine (opposite) and stands polishing the nameplate which carries the name of one of the oldest established hunts in the country. From his seat at Helmsley Castle, George Villiers, second Duke of Buckingham founded the Bilsdale hunt in 1668 and later died after 'catching a chill' whilst pursuing the sport in 1687. No. 62755 was erected at Darlington in July 1934 as LNER no. 226 and new to Scarborough. In the 1940s, the locomotive was at York and Scarborough before reaching Harrogate at the end of the decade. *The Bilsdale* remained there until 1956 when at Neville Hill for three months, moving on to Selby where the last two years in traffic passed. Both photographs courtesy *Yorkshire Post Newspapers*

Above NO. 62756 – YORK STATION

Scarborough's no. 62756 *The Brocklesby* is light engine at the south end of a relatively deserted York station 13th April 1957. The engine arrived at the depot in July 1951 and remained until condemned during April 1958. As LNER no. 230, the locomotive's first allocation was to Bridlington in August 1934. By the following year, a transfer to Hull Botanic Gardens occurred and at the end of the decade Neville Hill welcomed no. 62756. This comprised the period up to Scarborough taking the engine. Photograph by Bill Reed.

Opposite above and below NO. 62757 – HULL BOTANIC GARDENS SHED

LNER no. 238 *The Burton* became LNER no. 2757 in May 1946 and the BR number was used from August 1948. As seen previously, the latter often replaced the original and second numbers on the works plate, yet this has not occurred at this time (see image opposite below). *The Burton* is in the yard at Hull Botanic Gardens shed on 10th July 1949 and had been at Darlington for attention earlier in the year, though a general was not carried out until late summer 1950 when the change would perhaps take place. No. 62757 only had two allocations – Bridlington and Hull Botanic Gardens. New to the former in August 1934, the switch took place in April 1935. *The Burton* was later condemned in December 1957. Both photographs by T.B. Owen courtesy of Colour-Rail.

NO. 62759 – HARROGATE STARBECK SHED

Around 1958, no.62759 *The Craven* is in store at Harrogate shed. The engine returned to service and transferred to Hull. Photograph by Bill Reed.

Above NO. 62759 – PICKERING STATION

At Pickering station on 4th August 1950 is no. 62759 *The Craven*. The engine has both the York shed code on the smokebox door and the name on the buffer beam. Photograph by M.J. Reade courtesy of Colour-Rail.

Below NO. 62758 – YORK STATION

No. 62758 *The Cattistock* has a local train at York station on 13th April 1957. Shunting goods wagons on the right is Worsdell J72 Class 0-6-0T no. 68724. Photograph by Bill Reed.

Opposite above NO. 62761 – SELBY STATION

The Leeds & Selby Railway was the first to reach the latter town at the end of September 1834. A terminus was opened at the quayside and operational for six years before the Hull & Selby Railway arrived from the north, crossing the River Ouse to meet the L&SR at a new station constructed to the west of the original in 1840. As traffic grew to the end of the century, this station had to be rebuilt twice – during the early 1870s when the route between Doncaster and York was diverted via Selby, and again in the early 1890s, at which time the bridge over the Ouse was replaced. The 12.30 local from Hull is just crossing the swing bridge behind no. 62761 *The Derwent* on 5th April 1957. From 1983, Selby station has served only local traffic as the ECML was diverted in 1983. Photograph by B.W.L. Brooksbank.

Opposite below NO. 62760 – DARLINGTON

No. 62760 *The Cotswold* has arrived in Darlington for scrapping on 26th October 1959 just a few days after withdrawal. Photograph by D.J. Dippie.

Below NO. 62759 – SCARBOROUGH SHED

The crew of no. 62759 *The Craven* are utilising a water column at Scarborough shed in the mid-1950s. Amongst the final 25 D49s ordered, as LNER no. 274, the locomotive was new in late August 1934 and paired with a Group Standard tender. This had a 4,200-gallon water capacity, compared with the 4,125 gallons of the ex-NER tenders fitted and 4,000 of the ex-GCR. The Group Standard tenders of the last 25 engines were also fitted with vacuum brake reservoirs at the rear next to the water filler hole and this is just visible below the column spout. A water pick-up scoop was present on all and this was of a modified design to improve contact with the water in the troughs, with a further aim of reducing wastage. No. 62759 was Scarborough-allocated from new to November 1940 and again June 1943-March 1945. Photograph courtesy Rail-Online.

Below NO. 62762 – DARLINGTON WORKS

A death sentence has been passed on no. 62762 *The Fernie*. The locomotive was dispatched from Scarborough to Darlington Works for attention in October 1960 though the case was declared terminal soon after. Interestingly, at the last general repair in 1957 a new boiler was fitted, being one of eleven spare boilers built at the start of the 1950s for use with the class. The diagram 97 boiler was interchangeable with the J38 Class and some of these found use on those engines following withdrawal of D49 locomotives. This does not appear to be the case with boiler no. 27826 fitted to no. 62762. Just the chassis of the engine is seen here at Darlington Works on 22nd October, along with that of Worsdell J27 Class no. 65882, which returned to traffic and survived to the end of steam in the North East during September 1967. Photograph by D.J. Dippie.

Above NO. 62762 – ARTHINGTON

With two collisions in this engine's history, no. 62762 *The Fernie* is perhaps lucky to still be in traffic here. The first occurred in August/September 1946 whilst employed at Neville Hill shed and Darlington had the engine back in traffic after six weeks in the shops. During July/August 1948 a second collision took place and saw no. 62762 out of traffic until early November. Thankfully, the D49s remained free from being involved in a major accident though several appear to have been involved in minor mishaps. A visually dramatic one recorded on 27th May 1958 involved no. 62703 *Hertfordshire* which descended into the turntable pit at Bridlington. For this embarrassing calamity, no. 62703 was condemned soon after. No. 62762 has been captured at Arthington with an unidentified Gresley A3 during the early 1950s. The pair are at the head of a Liverpool-Newcastle express. Photograph courtesy *Yorkshire Post Newspapers*.

Above **NO. 62763**

In late September 1934 no. 359 *The Fitzwilliam* was completed at Darlington and initial employment was found at York. This went on for nearly 14 years when a move to Harrogate took place. From September 1959 to January 1961 no. 62763 (renumbered in October 1949) was housed at Hull Dairycoates. Possibly with a Raven 4-6-0, no. 62763 is piloting an express through an unidentified location, likely during the mid-1950s. Photograph courtesy *Yorkshire Post Newspapers*.

Opposite **NO. 62763 – LEEDS CITY STATION**

An express destined for Harrogate and Ripon exits the environs of Leeds City station in the mid-1950s with no. 62763 *The Fitzwilliam*. The area immediately west of the station was a particularly complex series of junctions and connections. Curving away on the right here is the line to Wortley (Canal Junction), whilst just further on was Leeds Junction to Holbeck engine shed, Hunslet (goods yard and station) and the south (Normanton, Pontefract, Sheffield, etc). The line continued on through Whitehall Junction to Holbeck where the westward lines met – Armley, Pudsey, Bradford, Halifax, etc – and those northward to Shipley and Skipton, as well as Harrogate, Ripon and Northallerton. Photograph by Kenneth Field from Rail Archive Stephenson courtesy Rail-Online.

Above NO. 62764 – SCARBOROUGH SHED

Although a black-and-white image, a red background to the nameplate appears to feature here on no. 62764 *The Garth*. Taking water at Scarborough shed in 1952, the locomotive was always attached to a Group Standard tender. Photograph courtesy Rail Photoprints.

Opposite page NO. 62763 – DARLINGTON SCRAPYARD

Two views of no. 62763 *The Fitzwilliam* in the scrapyard at Darlington on 13th February 1961. The one above provides a glimpse into the cab. Off to the left is the screw reverse wheel which reappeared for the rotary cam engine following complaints in Scotland of the steam reverse fitted to the original piston valve engines. The wheel controlled the reversing shaft which ran along the left-hand side of the engine to a set of bevel gears connected to the reversing mechanism. This was a worm wheel rack and pinion system which moved the camshaft laterally. The rotary motion of the camshaft was obtained on the opposite side of the locomotive and seen here connected to the leading driving wheel. In the second image, no. 62763's nameplate is seen without the fox and the works plate has also been removed. Both photographs by D.J. Dippie

Above **NO. 62765 – HULL**
Near Hull Paragon station on 7th August 1960 is no. 62765 *The Goathland*. The locomotive had under six months left in service before condemned. Photograph by Bill Reed.

Opposite above **NO. 62764**
Whilst the performance of the rotary cam D49s was adequate, this was not optimal owing to the limitations of the valve gear's five settings. With no. 365 *The Morpeth*, the LNER attempted to address this with an infinitely variable camshaft, yet this proved problematic and had to be removed early because of the war. British Railways resurrected the project and no. 62764 *The Garth* was equipped with the arrangement and after running in was sent to the locomotive testing station at Rugby – incidentally a project spearheaded by Gresley. No. 62764 performed well on the plant and in service, yet the modifications made to the original equipment posed difficulties, though these could have been rectified. *The Garth* appears to have retained the modified valve gear to withdrawal. The engine has an express at an unidentified location in the mid-1950s. Photograph courtesy Rail Photoprints.

Opposite below **NO. 62764 – YORK STATION**
On 21st July 1951, a light engine movement passes the Scarborough platforms at York station. No. 62764 *The Garth* is the locomotive, which was three weeks into an allocation to Leeds Neville Hill, with the depot's '50B' code on the door here. Originally based at Gateshead, the locomotive was approaching the end of the allocation there when fitted with the infinitely variable camshaft in late 1948. In the following year no. 62764 moved on to Scarborough after the tests were concluded. Photograph by B.W.L. Brooksbank.

Above NO. 62766 – BRIDLINGTON SHED

As mentioned, under BR the D49s soon became superfluous in certain areas and transfers took place to outlying sheds not previously associated with the class. No. 62766 *The Grafton* was one of several to be dispatched to Bridlington in the early 1950s and was mainly employed there through to June 1956 when taking a berth at Botanic Gardens depot. Two years later Bridlington shed closed, after more than 60 years serving locomotives. This was the third building erected for stabling, replacing a two-road building from the 1870s, which in turn had superseded the first shed built by the York & North Midland Railway in the 1840s. The shed was originally on the east side of Station Road bridge, whilst the second and third structures stood on the west side. No. 62766 is outside the shed in the early 1950s. Photograph by P.J. Hughes courtesy of Colour-Rail.

Opposite page NO. 62765 – DARLINGTON SCRAPYARD

Behind no. 62763 *The Fitzwilliam* in Darlington scrapyard on 13th February 1961 is no. 62765 *The Goathland*. Both had been condemned at Hull Dairycoates shed on 16th January 1961. Interestingly, both had 'officially' arrived at the depot on 13th September 1959. A further point of interest is the nameplates have been similarly shorn of their adornment and the works plate removed. Both photographs by D.J. Dippie.

Above NO. 62767 – BRIDLINGTON STATION

As with the majority of other LNER engines, Ross 'Pop' safety valves were fitted to the diagram 97 boiler used by the D49s. Specifically, the pair were each 2½ in. diameter and set to lift around a pressure of 180 lb per sq. in. On some of the early D49s, a base plate was present underneath the safety valves, though was omitted from the remainder. No. 62767 *The Grove* would not have carried this from new as LNER no. 367, nor has the fixture here at Bridlington station in the mid-1950s. The locomotive is viewed from Station Road bridge and has a local train likely bound for Hull. Bridlington had opened as the end of the first section of the York & North Midland line from Hull in October 1846 and the company later extended through to Seamer, meeting the Scarborough line. Photograph courtesy Rail-Online.

Below NO. 62767 – COTTINGHAM STATION

In 1951, no. 62767 *The Grove* passes Cottingham station with a local train in 1951. The year marked the fifth anniversary of a move from Gateshead to Botanic Gardens. The locomotive was at the latter through to withdrawal in October 1958. Gateshead received no. 62767 when constructed at Darlington in November 1934. The second LNER number, no. 2767, was applied from November 1946 when a general repair was completed at Darlington, whilst at the next general, though not the succeeding visit, BR number no. 62767 was used. *The Grove* referred to the meet at Retford, Nottinghamshire, which has since joined with The Rufford – a name carried by no. 62771. Photograph courtesy Rail Photoprints.

Above NO. 62768 – HARROGATE STATION

When Edward Thompson became Chief Mechanical Engineer of the LNER following the death of Sir Nigel Gresley in 1941, he set himself the task of streamlining the motive power of the company going forward. As the Second World War was in full swing, Thompson was restricted in how to enact these plans. One of his main aims was to improve performance and reduce maintenance. As the rotary cam D49s were in the minority, one was chosen to be rebuilt with a view to treating the remaining engines in a similar manner. No. 365 *The Morpeth* was in Darlington at the time and was fitted with two inside cylinders using piston valves and Stephenson motion. This transformation took 18 months between February 1941 and August 1942. When returned to traffic, several trials took place which ultimately found no. 365 unequal to other 4-4-0s, as well as piston valve D49s. No. 365 saw out the war at Leeds Neville Hill and just before Nationalisation moved to Harrogate. A year before this, the number became 2767 and in late summer 1948 the BR number was used. The locomotive is at Harrogate station on 29th November 1951 with crew posing happily for the camera. A year later the scene had changed considerably, with *The Morpeth* damaged during a shunting operation and subsequently withdrawn, though the tender was saved and reused with no. 62758 *The Cattistock*. Photograph courtesy *Yorkshire Post Newspapers*.

Opposite above NO. 62769 – YORK STATION

No. 62769 *The Oakley* is at the south end of York station in July 1950. The locomotive was Scarborough-allocated from May 1948 to September 1958 when withdrawn. Photograph by Geoffrey Oates.

Opposite below NO. 62769 – SCARBOROUGH STATION

In the 1950s, no. 62769 *The Oakley* is with a local train at Scarborough station. Photograph courtesy Rail-Online.

Above NO. 62771 – EDINBURGH HAYMARKET SHED

Blaydon shed was a late addition to the North Eastern Railway infrastructure when built to the west of Newcastle at the turn of the century. The main duties found for locomotives there were for goods trains, mineral traffic and shunting in local yards, whilst local passenger duties were also undertaken. The latter mainly saw the engines on the Newcastle-Carlisle line, particularly on to the Border Counties Railway route which left the latter at Hexham to snake north-westward to the Waverley Route at Riccarton Junction. Under the LNER, these trains were worked by North British Railway D31 Class 4-4-0s and NER Class D20s. When these became out of date after the war, two D49s were sent to Blaydon depot to take up the role. One was no. 62747 *The Percy* and the other no. 62771 *The Rufford*. The latter has reached further than the normal sphere of operation to Edinburgh Haymarket on 28th August 1954 and is seen in the shed yard. The D49s were at Blaydon until 1956 when the Border Counties line ceased taking passenger trains, though freight remained active to 1958. No. 62771 moved on to York in June 1956 and was operational there until October 1958. Photograph by David Anderson courtesy Rail Photoprints.

Opposite NO. 62770 – YORK STATION

The 12.42 Leeds to Scarborough service approaches York station from the south on 9th September 1958. The locomotive is no. 62770 *The Puckeridge* of Scarborough shed. As no. 368, the engine's career began in December 1934 at Leeds and this lasted 14 years until transferred to the aforementioned after Nationalisation. At this time British Railways was still in the midst of determining a numbering scheme and this led to an interim system being used. A prefix was provided before the number and in the case of ex-LNER locomotives, this was an 'E'. Just five D49s received this before 60,000 was added to the existing numbers. As no. E2770, *The Puckeridge* was amongst this select band, which also included: no. E2713 *Aberdeenshire*; no. E2718 *Kinross-shire*; no. E2736 *The Bramham Moor*; no. E2773 *The South Durham*. No. 62770 was applied to the locomotive from November 1949, at which time a general repair was carried out and a newly constructed boiler was fitted. The locomotive remained at Scarborough for another year and was briefly at Selby and York before sent for scrap in September 1959. Photograph by L. Rowe courtesy of Colour-Rail.

Above NO. 62771 – RICCARTON JUNCTION
The Border Counties Railway ran between the Newcastle-Carlisle line at Hexham and Riccarton on the Carlisle to Edinburgh – 'Waverley' – route. Approaching Riccarton Junction with a local train on 27th May 1953 is no. 62771 *The Rufford*. Photograph courtesy Rail Photoprints.

Opposite NO. 62772 – LEEDS CITY STATION
In December 1952, no. 62772 *The Sinnington* departs from Leeds City station, likely with an express for Harrogate, where the engine was employed at the time. This was the case between January 1948 and June 1956. Photograph courtesy *Yorkshire Post Newspapers*.

Above NO. 62773 – HARROGATE STARBECK SHED

The Group Standard tender of no. 62773 *The South Durham* is one of the later versions with flush sides and vacuum reservoir mounted at the rear on the right-hand side. The locomotive is outside Harrogate Starbeck shed on 20th May 1951. Allocated there at this time, no. 62773 was on the roster between December 1947 and June 1957. Photograph courtesy Rail-Online.

Opposite NO. 62774 – YORK

South of York, no. 62774 *The Staintondale* approaches with an express in 1954. At the end of the year a move from York to Harrogate occurred. Photograph courtesy Rail Photoprints.

Opposite above **NO. 62775 – HARROGATE STARBECK**
A local train passes through Starbeck, Harrogate, in 1956 behind no. 62775 *The Tynedale*. Coupled to the original flush-sided Group Standard tender-type is a clerestory carriage. Photograph courtesy Rail Photoprints.

Opposite below **NO. 62775 – DONCASTER STATION**
Simmering under the derelict platform canopies at Doncaster station is no. 62775 *The Tynedale*. In February 1935, the locomotive was the last D49 into traffic and later in the year was one of two poppet valve engines (the other was no. 292 *The Southwold*) tested against no. 251 *Derbyshire* with piston valves. The results favoured the latter in terms of fuel consumption and ease of operation. Following this conclusion, the experiment with the infinitely variable camshaft was instigated involving no. 365 *The Morpeth*. Photograph by Geoff Warnes.

Below **NO. 62775 – DARLINGTON SHED**
Standing at Darlington shed in ex-works condition in the early 1950s is no. 62775 *The Tynedale*. With the '50B' shed code on the smokebox door, the date is before September 1956 when a transfer from Neville Hill to Selby took place. From their introduction, the D49 class members were predominantly maintained by their respective areas: North East at Darlington; Scottish at Cowlairs, Glasgow. For a few years in the war, all D49s were sent to Cowlairs for repair before a return was made to the original arrangement. No. 62775 visited Cowlairs twice – in 1944 and 1946. Photograph by P.J. Hughes courtesy of Colour-Rail.

BIBLIOGRAPHY

Allen, C.J. *Titled Trains of Great Britain.* 1983.

Banks, Steve and Clive Carter. *LNER Passenger Trains and Formations 1923-1967: The Principal Services.* 2013.

Bolger, Paul. *BR Steam Motive Power Depots: North Eastern Region.* 2009.

British Rail Main Line Gradient Profiles.

Griffiths, Roger and Paul Smith. *The Directory of British Engine Sheds and Principal Locomotive Servicing Points: 2 North Midlands, Northern England and Scotland.* 2000.

Hoole, K. *A Regional History of the Railways of Great Britain Volume 4: The North East.* 1974.

Hoole, K. *North Eastern Locomotive Sheds.* 1972.

Knox, Harry. *Haymarket Motive Power Depot, Edinburgh: 1842-2010.* 2011.

Quick, Michael. *Railway Passenger Stations in Great Britain: A Chronology.* 2009.

RCTS. *Locomotives of the LNER – Part 4: Tender Engines – Classes D25 to E7.* 1968.

Walmsley, Tony. *Shed by Shed Part Three: North Eastern.* 2010.

Walmsley, Tony. *Shed by Shed Part Four: Scottish.* 2011.

Yeadon, W.B. *Yeadon's Register of LNER Locomotives Volume Ten: Gresley D49 and J38 Classes.* 2001.

Also available from Great Northern

The Last Years of Yorkshire Steam

The Golden Age of Yorkshire Railways

Gresley's A3s

Peppercorn's Pacifics

London Midland Steam 1948-1966

The Last Years of North East Steam

British Railways Standard Pacifics

Western Steam 1948-1966

The Last Years of North West Steam

Gresley's V2s

Southern Steam 1948-1967

Yorkshire Steam 1948-1967

Gresley's A4s

Gresley's B17s

The Last Years of West Midlands Steam

East Midlands Steam 1950-1966

Thompson's B1s

The Glorious Years of the LNER

Scottish Steam 1948-1967

The Last Years of London Steam

North East Steam 1948-1968

visit *www.greatnorthernbooks.co.uk* for details.